Natalia Bonner

BEGINNER'S GUIDE TO
Free-Motion
QUILTING

Professional Quality Results on Your Home Machine

50+ Visual Tutorials to Get You Started

BONUS
6 Modern Quilt Projects

stashBOOKS®
an imprint of C&T Publishing

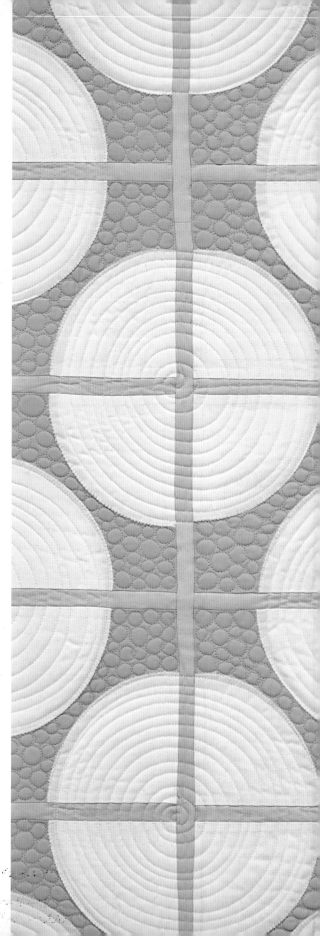

Publisher: Amy Marson

Creative Director: Gailen Runge

Art Director/Book Designer:
Kristy Zacharias

Editor: Cynthia Bix

Technical Editors: Carolyn Aune and
Priscilla Read

Page Layout Artist: April Mostek

Production Coordinator: Jenny Davis

Production Editor: S. Michele Fry

Illustrator: Mary Flynn

Photography by Christina Carty-Francis
and Diane Pedersen of C&T Publishing,
Inc., unless otherwise noted

Published by Stash Books, an imprint of C&T Publishing, Inc., P.O. Box 1456, Lafayette,
CA 94549

Library of Congress Cataloging-in-Publication Data

Bonner, Natalia, 1982-

Beginner's guide to free-motion quilting : 50+ visual tutorials to get you started-profes-
sional-quality results on your home machine / Natalia Bonner.

pages cm

ISBN 978-1-60705-537-2 (soft cover) 51155892 4/13

1. Patchwork--Patterns. 2. Machine quilting--Patterns. I. Title.

TT835.B626 2012

746.46--dc23

2011050325

Printed in China

10 9 8 7 6 5 4 3 2

Dedication

This book is dedicated to the women in my life who I believe passed this love of quilting on to me. My great-grandmother Ella, on whose birthday I was born in 1982, was a traditional quilter who traced all of her pieces from a cardboard template and cut them out with scissors. All of her quilts were made with scraps from old clothing. My grandma LaRae wanted to be a quilter, but because she was severely crippled with arthritis, she was unable to quilt as much as she would have liked. My grandma Emmy is a hand quilter who puts hours and hours of time into her quilts. My grandpa refers to her as a "topper," because she makes beautiful quilt tops and then stores them away under a bed until she has time to quilt them. Recently, she has let me machine quilt a few of her beautiful quilts.

My mom, Kathleen, sewed for my sister and me when we were growing up. She made us everything from our underwear to our swimming suits to the quilts on our beds. All the time I spent as a child watching her as she worked has influenced my life more than she can know.

Thank you to all of these women for teaching me and inspiring me. The skills and patience I learned from you as a child have now become the glue that keeps me in such close contact with cousins, aunts, and friends.

Acknowledgments

Special thanks to my whole family, but most of all to my mom, Kathleen Whiting. She has encouraged me and supported me from the day I got the crazy idea to leave my "real" job and pursue a career as a machine quilter. Thanks to my husband, Brad, and daughter, Chesney, for being patient with me day and night with my crazy quilting projects.

To Ashlee Woolf, Ilene Peterson, Vicki Christensen, and everyone else who helped me piece the quilts in this book—I could not have done all this without your help.

To everyone who reads my blog and attends quilt guilds with me—you have inspired and encouraged me more than you can imagine. Lissa Alexander and Angela Yosten— you saw something in me when I submitted my first Moda Bake Shop project.

To Moda Fabrics, Robert Kaufman Fabrics, and Riley Blake Designs for providing me with beautiful fabrics for this book.

To all the staff at C&T Publishing and Stash Books—you believed in me. To Susanne Woods for encouraging me to make my dreams come true. And to Cynthia Bix, Diane Pederson, and everyone else on my C&T book team—thanks so much for all of your hard work and for holding my hand all the way through.

CONTENTS

INTRODUCTION

I've always liked to sew and craft, but for a long time I had no idea of the potential for creativity in making quilts. When it came to quilting, I was stumped about what to do once I had my piece all sewn together. I had no idea that I could actually machine quilt and finish my quilts in really creative ways on my home sewing machine.

I had been working as a dental assistant for several years when I found out I was pregnant with my first child. I decided that I was going to quit my job and stay at home full time. Once home, I began spending more and more time making simple projects such as placemats and table runners and learning to machine quilt on them. I loved the feeling of satisfaction that came with finishing these fun, smaller projects. After I felt like I had mastered placemats and table runners, I moved onto quilting whole quilts.

I love to piece quilts as well as to quilt them. When the opportunity came to write this book about machine quilting, I thought, "You can't have one without the other!" I wanted to write a book that would include both machine quilting and piecing, and the result is this book.

This book has three main sections. In Focus on Quilting (page 7), you'll find everything you need to know to machine quilt, from fabrics and needles to batting and thread, plus tutorials on quilting 50 different quilting patterns. Once you feel comfortable with your quilting techniques, turn to Six Quilt Projects to Make (page 90) and choose a quilt to piece or appliqué—then quilt it, too! Finally, in Quilting Patterns (page 124), you'll find simple patterns to copy and use, from loops to detailed feathers.

Whether you are new to machine quilting or already have some basic machine quilting experience, I hope this book inspires you to look beyond the basics, to think beyond your comfort zone, and to enjoy the journey.

FOCUS ON QUILTING

In this section, you'll find all the basics about machine quilting, from choosing thread, batting, and fabrics to the ABC's of stitching on your quilt top. Then you'll have a chance to try your skills with more than 50 illustrated tutorials for stitching allover quilting, quilting borders and sashing, and adding background fillers, as well as quilting on individual blocks and on appliqué.

Machine Quilting BASICS

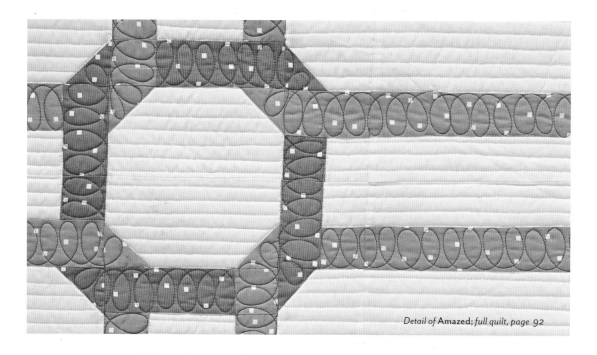

Detail of **Amazed**; *full quilt, page 92*

Many people are intimidated by the idea of machine quilting, but if you give it a try and take some time to practice, you'll find that it's actually easy to do. Not only that, but it's also creative and fun, and it gives you so much control over the final look of your quilt.

There are two basic kinds of machine quilting—*straight line* and *free motion*. Many people start out by doing straight-line quilting. For this, you use a walking foot, pictured in Machine Feet (page 9). This foot feeds the layers of your quilt evenly under the needle at the same time that the machine's feed dogs feed it from underneath. You can use this foot to quilt parallel lines, grids, and diagonal lattice patterns. Straight-line patterns are easy to quilt and can be great fillers on a solid background, as shown in the detail of *Amazed*.

This book focuses on free-motion quilting, which allows you to quilt any kind of pattern you wish, from swirls and circles to flowers and feathers. It's a little like drawing on the quilt top with the needle. For information about the special machine foot you will need for free-motion quilting, see Machine Feet (page 9).

TOOLS AND MATERIALS

Tools and materials for machine quilting are pretty simple: You need a sewing machine in good working order, with free-motion capability. You also need thread, needles, batting, and your quilt! Here you'll find useful information about choosing among the many options within these simple categories. For recommended online sources, see Resources (page 175).

Sewing Machine

Machine quilting can be done successfully on most conventional home machines, as long as the machine has a free-motion foot. I currently have a Bernina Aurora 440 and a Bernina Aurora 450. It's also helpful to have an extension table for your machine; this accessory creates a larger working area than the standard machine bed offers.

MACHINE FEET

When free-motion quilting, lower the machine's feed dogs (the little teeth that move the fabric from underneath) and use a free-motion foot that lets you move the quilt layers freely under the needle. Free-motion feet for different machines vary (they are made in assorted shapes and can be metal or clear plastic) and can be called by different names, such as darning foot. A foot with a clear plastic sole is great because it provides improved visibility.

My Bernina has a BSR (Bernina Stitch Regulator), which is a foot that controls the sewing speed and helps regulate the length between stitches as you move the fabric. I really like the BSR foot because no matter what speed I move the fabric under the needle, my stitches always look about the same length.

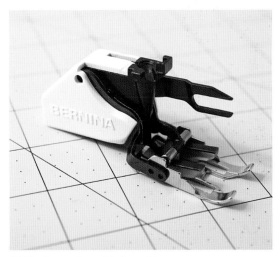

Walking foot used in straight-line quilting

Free-motion feet used in free-motion quilting

Needles

Two different types of needles can be used for quilting on a home sewing machine—a quilting needle and a topstitch needle. A quilting needle has a slim, tapered point and slightly stronger shaft for stitching through fabric layers and across intersecting seams. However, most machine quilting can be done using a topstitch needle, which has an extra-sharp point and eye and a larger groove to accommodate heavier threads. I always use a titanium-coated topstitching needle. Titanium-coated needles last up to five times as long as regular needles. I prefer the needles made by Superior Threads, but you can choose from the many others that are available.

It is important that you have the correct size of topstitch needle for the thread you are using. I recommend three sizes for quilting: the #80/12 for piecing and machine quilting with fine thread, the #90/14 for machine quilting with medium-weight thread, and the #100/16 for machine quilting with heavy-weight thread.

Finally, be sure to use a sharp needle. Stitching dulls the needle after a while, so I recommend changing your needle often to get the best results.

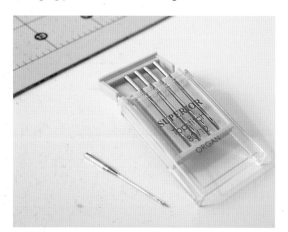

Other Useful Supplies

Gloves made especially for quilting can make machine quilting easier. These gloves have gripper dots on the fingers and palms that help you hold the quilt sandwich securely to guide it under the presser foot. I like Machingers, but there are other brands, too.

Quilter's safety pins, which are curved for easier insertion into the quilt layers, are a great choice for pin basting, as described in Layering and Basting (page 17). But you can use regular safety pins instead.

Thread

Choosing the correct thread for machine quilting is very important. There are so many types and brands that it can be hard to choose. The most common types of thread suggested for machine quilting are cotton, polyester, and polyester-wrapped cotton.

I always use high-quality polyester thread by Superior Threads—Bottom Line in my bobbin and So Fine! as my top thread. But you can certainly try various brands and types to see which you prefer. You do not have to use only cotton thread on cotton fabric or only polyester thread on polyester. Just be sure to select high-quality thread.

Thread size is also a factor to consider. Although there is no single system for designating thread sizes, a very common system uses two numbers; for example, 50/3 is all-purpose sewing thread. The first number is the thread's "weight," and the second number indicates the number of plies in the thread. The higher the weight number, the finer the thread.

I prefer to machine quilt and piece with 50- or 60-weight polyester threads. I like the soft look of the finer thread. On occasion, when I want the thread to stand out, I use a heaver thread, such as 40-weight polyester.

When choosing thread colors, I recommend using the same color thread on top and bottom, especially when you are first learning to quilt. Some quilters get special effects by using different colors on the top and bottom threads, but matching the threads ensures better results.

Variegated threads, which combine more than one color in the same thread, are also very popular. Some have multiple colors that change every couple of inches, while others may just have two or three shades of one color. Variegated threads can add a whole different look to your quilting.

Note: Never use hand-quilting thread for machine quilting! Hand-quilting thread has a waxy coating that is not compatible with sewing machines.

Cotton thread is made by spinning cotton fibers together, and then pulling and twisting them into a narrow strand. Each strand is called a *ply*. Plies are twisted together to create stronger thread.

Polyester thread is a synthetic material. Polyester is spun together like cotton but generally has more stretch.

Polyester-wrapped cotton thread combines the stretch of polyester thread with the strength of cotton thread.

Batting

Batting—the "filling" between the quilt top and backing in the quilt "sandwich"—affects the look and feel of your quilt, as well as the way you quilt it.

Battings are held together in two different ways—bonded or needle punched. In bonded batting, the fibers are bonded together with a gluelike bonding agent. In needle-punched batting, the fibers are mechanically felted together by punching them with multiple needles.

Every batting comes with a manufacturer's recommendation for how much space you can leave between lines of quilting (how closely it must be quilted). When choosing a batting, it is important to know the recommended stitching distance.

When you are beginning to quilt, I recommend using Hobbs Heirloom 80/20 Cotton Blend batting, which is both lightly needle punched and bonded. When you become confident in your quilting, try different types of batting to achieve different looks. You have many options, depending on the look you want and how you will use the quilt.

Cotton/polyester batting is generally slightly loftier than 100% cotton and a little more breathable than 100% polyester. It also usually shrinks less than 100% cotton batting does. The recommended quilting distance is 2˝–4˝.

Cotton batting drapes well and softens with age, washing, and usage. It also shrinks and wrinkles the first time it is washed, which gives the quilt an antique look. The recommended quilting distance is up to 8˝.

Polyester batting is generally a loftier batting used for thick, puffy quilts. Polyester batting is lighter than cotton batting and is nonallergenic. However, it does not breathe like natural fibers do. Also, its high loft can make it very difficult to

use when machine quilting. The recommended quilting distance varies among different lofts and brands.

Wool batting is light, soft, and warm. Wool batting recovers better from being compressed than does any other fiber. It is also naturally flame resistant. However, wool batting can cause allergic reactions and must be protected from moths. The recommended quilting distance is up to 8˝.

Silk batting is lightweight, thin, and warm. It is generally used in quilted garments. Silk batting shrinks more than other battings, so you must be very careful when washing it. The recommended quilting distance is 3˝.

Bamboo batting is an environmentally friendly choice, because it comes from an extremely fast-growing plant that does not require fertilizers to grow. Bamboo batting drapes beautifully and is breathable and cool like cotton. However, it can be expensive. The recommended quilting distance is 8˝.

I prefer to use a cotton/polyester blend batting. My favorite brands are Quilters Dream Blend 70/30 (70% cotton, 30% polyester) and Hobbs Heirloom 80/20 Cotton Blend (80% cotton, 20% polyester).

You can buy batting by the yard from a roll or precut and packaged. I prefer batting from a roll. I find that prebagged batting is often hard to work with because the folds created in the bag often stay in the batting and will show up as creases in the quilt.

Most batting is white or off-white, which works with most quilt tops. However, if the colors in your quilt are very light, consider using a bleached white batting to prevent it from showing through. If the colors are dark, black battings are available.

A Word About Fabrics

If you're going to put time and creative energy into quilting, of course you want the actual quilt itself to be something you love and something that will last. So always use high-quality cotton fabrics to make your quilt top and backing. These fabrics are made with a higher thread count and tighter weave, so they will not wrinkle, fade, or wear out as easily as lower-quality fabrics do. Most high-quality cottons cannot be found in chain stores. I recommend purchasing fabric for your quilts from smaller, independently owned quilting stores or online independent quilt fabric retailers.

High-quality cottons have a pleasant luster, soft drape, and smooth "hand." The colors have generally been set, so prewashing is most often not necessary. I never prewash my fabrics, as I like the crisp look and feel of the unwashed fabrics. However, if you'd like a softer, more "used" look, you may want to prewash your quilt fabrics and then wash the quilt again after it is bound.

As far as fabric choice goes, I prefer to use a combination of prints and solids rather than all prints. Solid-color fabrics will really show off your machine quilting!

QUILTING TECHNIQUES

In this section, you'll find basic quilting tips to get you started. You may find that free-motion machine quilting can be discouraging at first, but it's really not hard! Just take your time and do plenty of practicing. Start small—on hot pads, mug rugs, or pillows—and then work your way up to quilts.

Layering and Basting

Begin by layering the quilt top, batting, and backing, and then basting them together. Cut the backing and batting 4˝ larger than the quilt top on all sides. Make sure that the quilt top is squared up, the top and backing are pressed, and all threads are clipped.

You will need a large, flat surface, such as a table or a clean floor or carpet. If you have a table larger than the quilt, lay out the quilt backing wrong side up on the table. Tape it down with masking tape, or use clamps to hold the backing flat. If you do not have a table large enough, clear an area on the floor. On tile or wood, you can use masking tape to tape the backing flat. If you are working on carpet, use T-pins to pin it flat.

Center and lay the batting flat on the backing; then center the quilt top right side up on top of the batting. Now you can begin to baste.

Basting can be done using safety pins or basting spray or by stitching by hand or machine. No matter which method you choose, it is very important that the layers lie flat and are positioned correctly. It's important to take the time to baste properly, as this will help ensure better results when machine quilting your quilt.

When spray basting, follow the instructions on the spray can to baste between each layer.

When basting by hand or machine, stitch a row horizontally, then vertically, and then diagonally across the quilt—using much longer than normal stitches—to create a single row each way. Then begin to fill in, making a grid across the quilt with stitched rows about 6˝ apart to evenly secure the quilt layers. If you are basting by hand, use long strands of light-colored thread and take very generous stitches so they can be easily removed when you're finished quilting. If basting by machine, use a walking foot and work from the center out in sections to create a grid.

For pin basting, use size #1 or #2 safety pins. Curved quilting pins work especially well. I recommend using approximately 75 pins for a crib-sized quilt and up to 350 pins for a queen-sized quilt. Start pinning at the center of the quilt, making sure to pin all three layers together and spacing the pins about a palm's-width apart. Pin outward horizontally and vertically, creating a gridlike pattern.

Getting Ready to Quilt

It is important that your sewing machine is located on a large table with good lighting and plenty of room to move the quilt as you stitch. Make sure the machine and chair are at a comfortable height for you. Put on the machine's extension table if it has one. You may want to put the machine on your kitchen table if the table is large, or set up an ironing board next to your sewing table so the quilt can drape over it. The more area you have to lay the quilt out flat as you sew, the easier it will be to maneuver.

Before starting to quilt, draw out your designs on paper. Try to draw continuous lines without stopping; this will help you get familiar with how you will need to move the quilt under the needle.

To get your machine ready for quilting, drop the feed dogs and attach a free-motion foot, as described in Machine Feet (page 9). If you work with the BSR foot, you will have a little bit better control over your stitch length and tension. I like my stitches to be secure, so generally with a BSR, I set my stitch to 10 or 11 stitches per inch. If you are not working with a BSR foot, it won't matter what stitch length you set; instead, the speed with which you move the quilt under the needle will determine the stitch length. Getting the stitches even and the length you want is difficult when you first start free-motion quilting, but with practice, it gets easier.

THREAD TENSION

Good thread tension means that your stitching looks good on both sides of the quilt, with an equal amount of thread on the top and bottom and no loops. Loopy threads mean the tension is too loose; puckered and pulled threads mean it is too tight.

Adjusting tension can be very tricky because you may have to adjust both the top thread and the bobbin tension. Most newer machines have a recommended tension setting, but it's not always accurate, especially for machine quilting. You can easily change the top tension by adjusting your machine's tension gauge, but it is often the bobbin tension that makes all the difference. You can adjust the tension of most bobbins by turning the screw on the bobbin case. Check your owner's manual to see how to adjust both top and bobbin tensions on your machine.

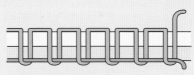

Top tension is too loose, or bobbin tension is too tight.

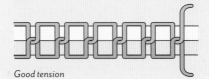

Top tension is too tight, or bobbin tension is too loose.

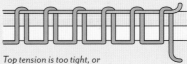

Good tension

Top tension gauge

Adjusting tension screw on bobbin case

Quilting a Sample

Begin by practicing and becoming familiar with free-motion quilting on your particular machine before you start quilting a full-size quilt. I recommend practicing on small 10˝ × 10˝ quilt sandwiches first.

Let's practice by quilting basic loops.

1. Turn to the Single Loop pattern (page 125) and refer to How to Use the Quilting Patterns (page 23) to trace it onto a 10˝ × 10˝ square of solid scrap fabric. Prepare the mini sandwich as described in Layering and Basting (page 17). If you pin baste, simply remove the pins as you go.

tip If you are worried about wasting thread or fabric, trace the pattern onto a sheet of paper. Unthread your machine and practice stitching on the paper. The lines you're quilting on paper will appear as perforations that will allow you to see how your technique is improving.

2. You'll start quilting in the center of one edge of the quilt and work out from there. Place the prepared quilt sandwich under the machine's presser foot.

3. Take a single stitch to bring the bobbin thread to the top, and then pull the top thread tight to pull up the bobbin thread loop to the top of the quilt. Take your top thread and loop it around the bottom thread, under the machine foot, to pull the entire bottom thread to the top. This way, both thread tails will stay on top, which will help you avoid a "bird's nest" of tangled threads.

4. Take a couple of small stitches in place to secure the thread; then cut off the thread tails.

5. Now you are ready to begin quilting. Start by moving the quilt around in a small loop, following the pattern lines. Take a single loop; then stitch along the line to the next loop. Get used to the feeling of moving the fabric backward, forward, and sideways under the foot. If you don't have a BSR foot to keep your stitches even, try to keep the fabric moving at a consistent pace to get the most even stitches. Figure A.

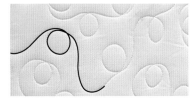

Figure A.

6. Stitch another single loop, but this time, go in the opposite direction, as the pattern indicates. Figure B.

7. Repeat Steps 5 and 6, alternating directions as shown. Figure C.

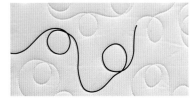

Figure B.

8. When you are ready to stop, take a couple of small securing stitches in place. Pull the quilt about 5˝ away from the needle, leaving a long thread tail. Clip the top thread close to the fabric. Now move the quilt back to the point where you stopped stitching, take a single stitch, and pull up the bobbin thread. It will be a loop; pull it up and clip the bobbin thread close to the fabric.

And that's it—you've done your first free-motion machine quilting! Just practice, practice, practice on as many mini quilt sandwiches as it takes for you to feel comfortable.

Figure C.

Quilting on a "Real" Quilt

When you're ready to stitch on a full-size quilt, you will have many options for quilting. You can do *allover quilting,* which means you quilt from edge to edge of the quilt without regard to block designs or borders. Allover quilting gives the quilt texture and adds an extra element of design. This is a great way to start, because you can just keep repeating a basic design.

Many machine quilters use a basic *stippling* design (also called *meandering*) to do allover quilting. Stippling is done in continuously curving lines that never cross. The lines can be fairly loose or tight (called microstippling). Although stippling is certainly a good way to begin, this book offers patterns that go beyond stippling to include loops, daisies, swirls, and more. They are all still easy to do, but more varied.

Detail of **Daisy Drop;** *full quilt, page 110*

STRAIGHT-LINE QUILTING

Straight-line quilting is very simple—it feels a lot like sewing straight seams. Use a walking foot; there is no need to lower the feed dogs. Prepare the quilt sandwich as for free-motion quilting, and practice on a small sample first to be sure the tension is adjusted correctly. Follow Steps 2–4 of Quilting a Sample (page 20) to begin stitching. Stitching parallel lines about ½˝ apart is a good way to begin. To keep the spacing even, some quilters like to use a stitch guide or arm. Others like to use narrow quilter's tape as a guide. When you come to the edge of the quilt, stitch right off the edge of the quilt top. The stitches will be secured under the binding after the quilt is completed.

Background fillers can be very similar to allover designs. Background fillers are great for adding dimension to a quilt. In this case, you quilt a fairly dense design on the quilt's background areas, around main pieced motifs or blocks. The more densely you quilt the background, the more other areas of the quilt will "pop."

After you have mastered allover quilting and background fillers, you can move on to *custom quilting*. Custom quilting means that you quilt different designs in blocks, borders, and sashing to give each area of the quilt a custom look. *Borders* and *sashing* are a great place to start the journey into custom quilting. In quilted borders and sashing, you add stitched designs tailored to fit into the strips; these add much more detail to a quilt. You also can quilt custom designs individually in quilt blocks. Custom quilting adds another dimension to the block, whether it is pieced, appliquéd, or plain.

You will find patterns and step-by-step instructions in this book for doing all of these kinds of quilting.

When quilting on a full-size quilt, use the same basic technique as described under Quilting a Sample (page 20). One main difference, however, is that when you place the quilt on your machine, you will need to roll the quilt from two sides toward the center so that you can hold the part being quilted flat and move it under the foot more easily. You can use large binder clips or bicycle slips or anything else that will help keep the sides rolled up as you work. Start quilting in the center of the quilt, and work from the center out in one direction. Then go back to the center and work out in the other direction.

Take a deep breath and relax! The more relaxed you are, the smoother your quilted designs will be. Soon you will develop a rhythm that will carry you through stitching over the entire quilt.

Squaring Up Your Quilt

After you have finished machine quilting the entire quilt, trim the edges of the quilt top, removing excess batting and backing. Even though you have made sure to square up the quilt top before machine quilting it, a quilt can often go somewhat out of square during quilting. Generally, I go ahead and bind my quilt; then if it still needs some squaring up, I do that after binding. If the quilt has gotten really out of square, you may want to try to square it up before binding. However, some piecing patterns will not allow for much squaring up.

To square up a quilt after quilting and binding, lay a piece of batting or a blanket a little larger than the quilt on a clean floor or carpet. Lay the finished quilt on top of the batting. Spray the entire surface with water so the quilt is well moistened. Using a yardstick or carpenter's square as a guide, gently pull and smooth the quilt top to straighten it. Tape it out square, or use T-pins, sticking them firmly right into the carpet to hold the quilt square. Leave the quilt like this overnight. I usually set up a small room fan and let it blow on the quilt all night long.

HOW TO USE THE QUILTING PATTERNS

Free-motion quilting means just that: You move the quilt freely under the needle to create designs. In Section Three, I've given you patterns to trace and use. However, these are intended just for practice. You can quilt by following the pattern as many times as you want on smaller pieces to get the hang of it. Then, when you are ready to work on a full quilt, you will be able to quilt the same design without using a pattern.

If you do choose to trace the pattern, you can either trace it onto the top fabric or cut out the pattern and draw around it. Be sure to trace it before you create the quilt sandwich. I usually trace allover patterns onto the fabric using a blue water-soluble marker. If you don't have access to a lightbox, you can place the top fabric over the pattern and tape it on a window for tracing. For block or detailed patterns, you may want to cut out the design shape and use the marker to trace around it on the fabric. Wait until you've quilted the entire piece before you rinse out the marker lines.

Allover QUILTING

Allover quilting means quilting the entire quilt top, edge to edge, with no regard to borders, blocks, or appliqué. The most important thing in allover quilting is to quilt your repeating pattern evenly over the whole quilt. You'll find instructions here for quilting fifteen different designs.

LOOPS

Loops are an easy and versatile allover quilting design. In this section, you will learn to make seven variations: Single and double loops and loops with daisies, poppies, leaves, hearts, and stars.

Single Loops

Pattern is on page 125.

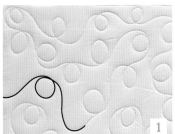

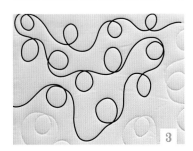

STEP 1. *Stitch a single loop, then meander a small distance.*

STEP 2. *Stitch another single loop, but this time, go in the opposite direction.*

STEP 3. *Repeat Steps 1 and 2, alternating directions, to cover the entire quilt.*

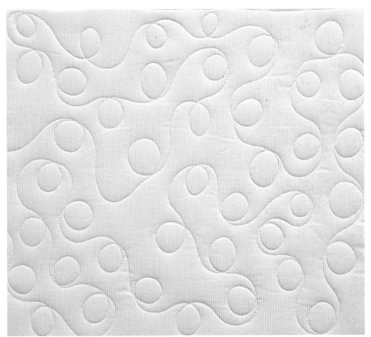

tip To fill an entire quilt, I like covering about 12˝ square spaces at a time. I fill in a 12˝ area and then move on to another 12˝ area. You don't have to work in exact 12˝ squares, but it helps to work in small areas to eventually cover a large area.

Double Loops

Pattern is on page 126.

When you become comfortable with the single loop, you can dress it up a little bit by making it a double loop.

STEP 1. *After you have created a loop as shown in Single Loops (page 25) and you are back to the beginning point, stitch a small loop inside the original loop.*

STEP 2. *Continue making single loops and adding a second loop inside each one as you go, covering the entire quilt in the same way you did for Single Loops.*

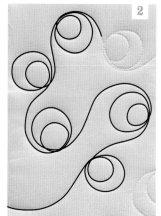

tip I generally space my loops about 3˝–4˝ apart. However, if you get to an area that needs more quilting, fill in that area as needed.

Loops and Daisies

Pattern is on page 127.

Once you have mastered the single loop, you can start adding to it. Start with a daisy.

STEP 1. *Stitch a couple of loops, as described in Single Loops (page 25).*

STEP 2. *Stitch to the spot where the daisy's center will be. Stitch back out in a slight arc to the top of the first flower petal, then stitch around the other way back to the center. Continue until you have 5 petals. When you arrive back at the original starting point, stitch a small circle in the center.*

STEP 3. *Exit the daisy on the opposite side from where you entered, and continue stitching loops—generally 2 or 3 loops between daisies—and adding daisies. Continue stitching to cover the entire quilt in the same way you did for Single Loops.*

Loops and Poppies

Pattern is on page 128.

Now try a poppy instead of a daisy. Poppies have more rounded petals.

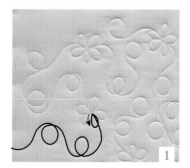

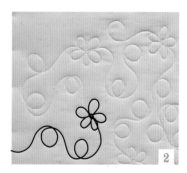

STEP 1. *Stitch a couple of loops, as described in Single Loops (page 25). Stitch to the spot where the poppy's center will be. Stitch a rounded line to the top of the first petal, and then stitch around the other way to the center point.*

STEP 2. *Continue until you have 5 nicely rounded petals. When you arrive back at your original starting point, stitch a small circle in the center.*

STEP 3. *Exit the poppy on the opposite side from where you entered. Continue stitching loops—generally 2 to 3 loops between poppies—and adding poppies to cover the quilt.*

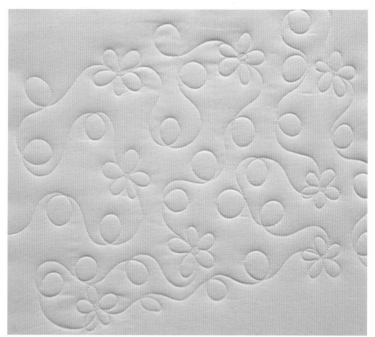

Loops and Leaves

Pattern is on page 129.

For a different look, add leaves to the loops instead of flowers.

STEP 1. *Stitch a couple of loops, as described in Single Loops (page 25). Stitch to the spot where you want the base of the leaf to be.*

STEP 2. *Stitch up the center to create a spine. Stop and come back down the spine to the base of the leaf.*

STEP 3. *Stitch a curved line around to the point of the leaf and then back down the opposite side to the base.*

STEP 4. *Continue quilting loops—generally 2 to 3 loops between each leaf—and adding leaves. For a nice overall look, make the leaves point in all directions off the loop "vines."*

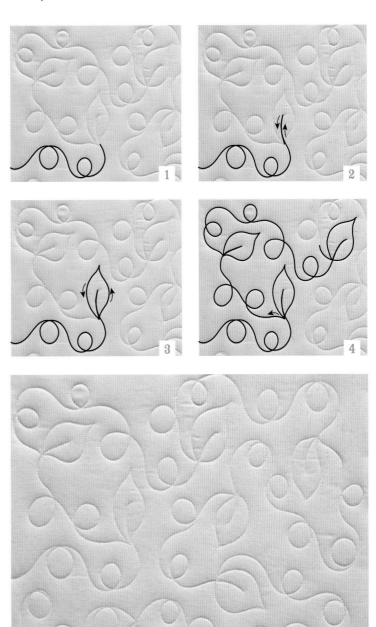

Loops and Hearts

Pattern is on page 130.

Hearts are a sweet addition to loops.

STEP 1. *Stitch a couple of loops, as described in Single Loops (page 25). From the last loop, stitch to a point that will be the center of the heart.*

STEP 2. *From the center point of the heart, stitch out to one side to form half of the heart; pivot and stitch back on a line that mirrors the first line, ending in the same place where you began.*

STEP 3. *Stitch away from the heart in the opposite direction and continue stitching loops in alternating directions, with a heart after every 2 to 3 loops. For a nice overall look, make the hearts point in various directions off the loop vines.*

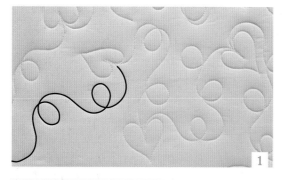

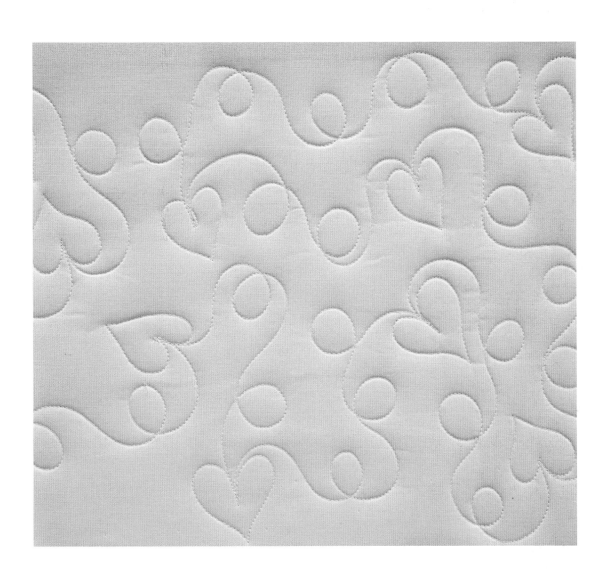

Loops and Stars

Pattern is on page 131.

These five-pointed stars have a charming, hand-drawn look.

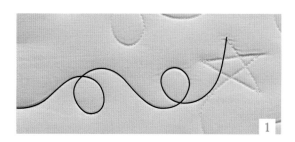

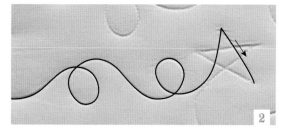

STEP 1. *Stitch a couple of loops, as described in Single Loops (page 25). Stitch to where you want point 1 of the star to be.*

STEP 2. *Stitch to point 2.*

STEP 3. *Stitch to point 3.*

STEP 4. *Stitch to point 4.*

STEP 5. *Stitch back to where you began point 5.*

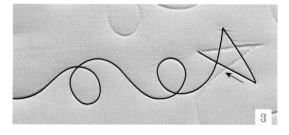

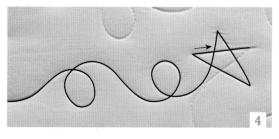

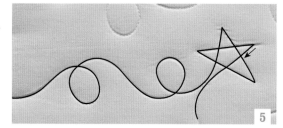

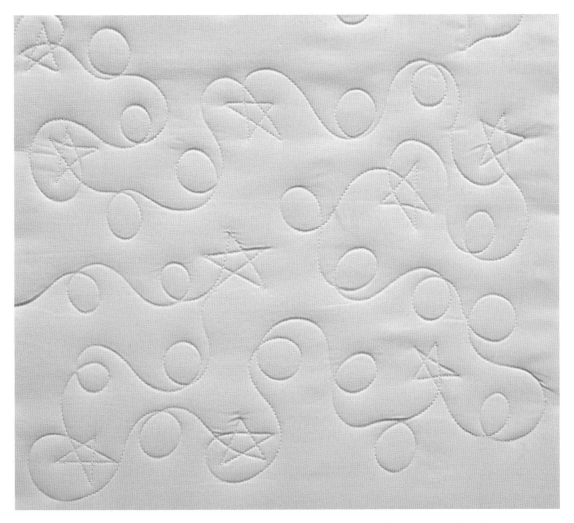

For the best results, enter and exit the star from opposite directions. Continue stitching loops—generally 2 to 3 between each star—and adding stars.

SWIRLS

Swirls are a little more complex than loops, but with practice they are fun to do and add a lot of detail and dimension to a quilt. In this section, you will learn to make five variations: swirls and swirls with daisies, poppies, half-daisies, and half-poppies.

Swirls

Pattern is on page 132.

STEP 1. *Start on an outside edge of the quilt, and stitch in a swirl motion that curls into the center, spacing lines approximately ½˝ apart.*

STEP 2. *When you reach the center, stop and stitch back out in a swirl motion; this will make the stitch lines about ¼˝ apart.*

STEP 3. *Repeat Steps 1 and 2 to create a second swirl that branches off the first.*

STEP 4. *After completing a couple of swirls, fill in with more swirls. Stitch around the swirl and create a point from which to fill in between 2 swirls. Continue filling in until the entire quilt surface is covered.*

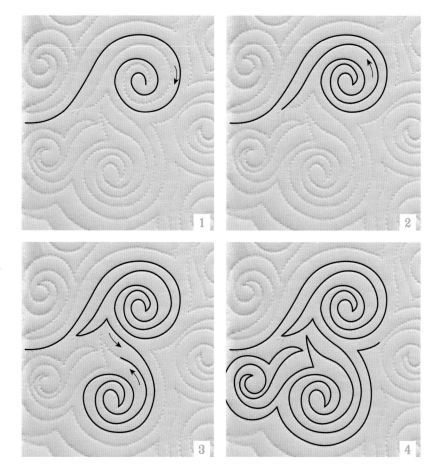

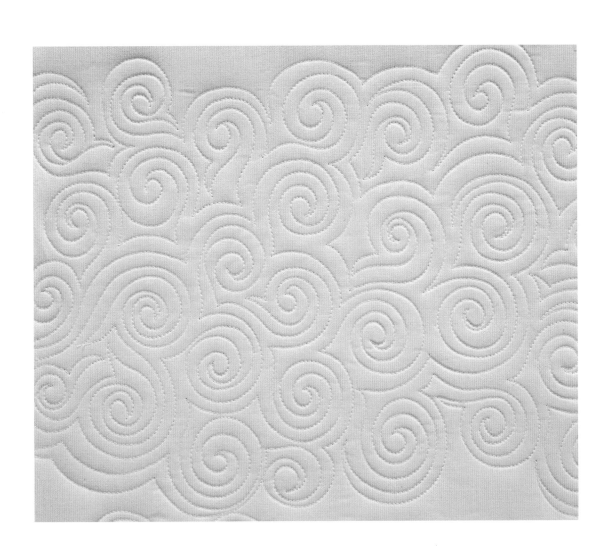

Swirls and Daisies

Pattern is on page 133.

When you've mastered the basic swirl, you can add flowers to it. Start with daisies.

STEP 1. *Stitch an area of swirls, as described in Swirls (page 34). Stitch a long stem that leads away from the swirl area.*

STEP 2. *Stitch a single swirl for the daisy center.*

STEP 3. *When you arrive back to your starting point at the end of the stem, stitch 6 pointed daisy petals all the way around the center swirl.*

STEP 4. *When you get about ¼˝ from the stem, stitch "echoes" of the petals all the way around the flower until you get about ¼˝ from the original stem. Stitch parallel to your original stem, about ¼˝ away, all the way back to the swirl section. Stitch more swirls to fill in around the stem and the daisy.*

> *tip* If you are having a hard time filling in the space with swirls, simply echo the previous swirls. The nice thing about swirls is that you can always add an echo or two to fill in and give your quilting a consistent look.

Repeat as many daisies among the swirls as you like!

Swirls and Poppies

Pattern is on page 134.

Poppies are another nice addition to swirl patterns.

STEP 1. *Stitch an area of swirls, as described in Swirls (page 34).*

STEP 2. *Stitch a long stem that leads away from the swirl area, and then stitch a single swirl for the poppy center.*

STEP 3. *When you arrive back at the starting stem, stitch 6 poppy petals all the way around the swirl.*

STEP 4. *When you get about ¼˝ from the stem, stitch an "echo" of the petals all the way around the flower until you get about ¼˝ from your original stem. Stitch about ¼˝ parallel to your original stem all the way back to your swirl section. Stitch more swirls to fill in around the stem and the poppy.*

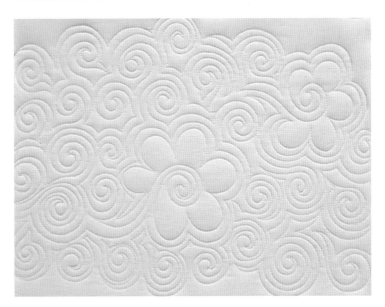

Repeat as many poppies among the swirls as you like!

Swirls and Half-Daisies

Pattern is on page 135.

Half-daisies among swirls give you a slightly different look from whole daisies.

STEP 1. *Stitch an area of swirls, as described in Swirls (page 34). Stitch a long stem that leads away from the swirl area, and then stitch a single swirl for the daisy center.*

STEP 2. *When you arrive back at the starting stem, stitch 3 daisy petals halfway around the swirl. At the end of the third petal, go back and echo the petals all the way around the flower until you get about ¼˝ away from your original stem. Stitch about ¼˝ parallel to the original stem all the way back to the swirl section. Stitch more swirls to fill in around the stem and the half-daisy.*

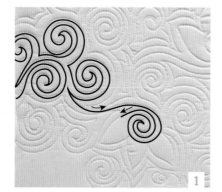

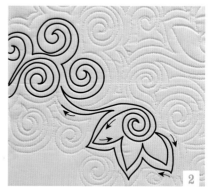

Repeat half-daisies among the swirls as often as desired.

Swirls and Half-Poppies

Pattern is on page 136.

Half-poppies among swirls give you a slightly different look from whole poppies.

STEP 1. *Stitch an area of swirls, as described in Swirls (page 34). Stitch a long stem that leads away from the swirl area, and then stitch a single swirl for the poppy center.*

STEP 2. *When you arrive back at the starting stem, stitch 3 poppy petals halfway around the swirl. At the end of the third petal, go back and echo the petals all the way around the flower until you get about ¼˝ away from the original stem. Stitch about ¼˝ parallel to the original stem all the way back to the swirl section. Stitch more swirls to fill in around the stem and the half-poppy.*

Repeat as many half-poppies among the swirls as you wish.

FEATHERS

Pattern is on page 137.

The feather pattern is a classic quilting design. Stitching feathers takes some practice, but the design is very forgiving. Use feathers to fill in open areas on your quilt top. Remember that these feathers are intended to be soft and flowing, not stiff.

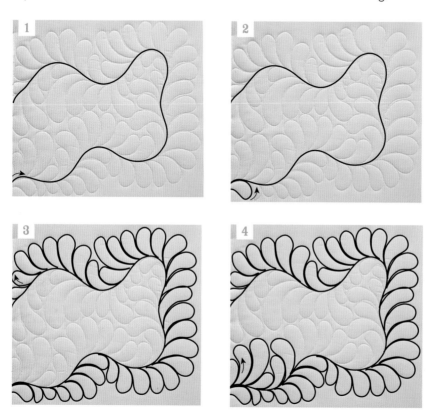

STEP 1. *Begin by stitching a long meandering line; this will be the "spine" of the feathers. Keep the spine 4˝ to 6˝ away from itself at all times.*

STEP 2. *To stitch the first feather, start at the end point of the spine, and stitch a single feather shape, returning to the original starting point of the feather.*

STEP 3. *To create the next feather, stitch back directly on top of the stitching until you are nearly to the top of the first feather, and then curve away to make the top of the second feather. Complete the second feather. Continue stitching in this way to make feathers all along one side of the spine, varying their size and keeping their edges close together. Stitch until you are back at the starting point.*

STEP 4. *Move onto the other side of the spine. Starting at the very bottom point, fill in with feathers that mirror those on the first side. These feathers do not have to be exactly the same size as the feathers on the opposite side, but try to keep them somewhat consistent overall.*

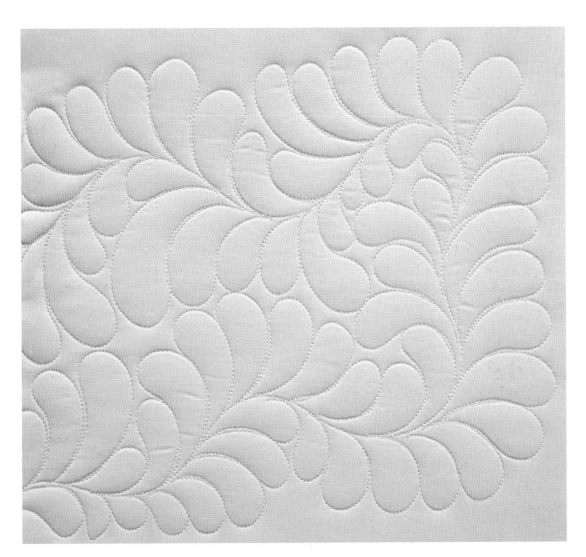

Most quilts have several spines of feathers.

FLAMES

Pattern is on page 138.

Flames are a dramatic design created using wavy lines.

STEP 1. *Beginning at the bottom, stitch a gentle wavy line straight up.*

STEP 2. *Come to a point and stitch another wavy line going down.*

STEP 3. *Continue to stitch wavy lines, packing them together densely. To achieve an effective allover flame design, make sure that all the flames are different lengths. Continue stitching the closely packed flames until you have covered the entire area.*

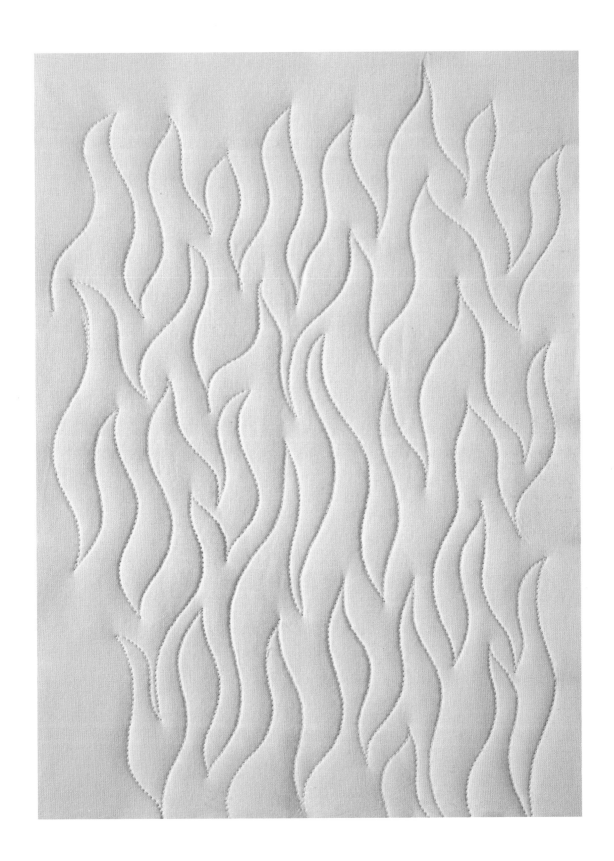

CIRCLES

Pattern is on page 139.

Simple spiral-stitched circles can lend a great modern look to your quilt, especially when you stitch them in varying sizes and connect them with straight lines.

STEP 1. *Start stitching a swirl, as described in Swirls (page 34), but keep the stitches about ¼˝ apart.*

STEP 2. *Swirl into the inside of the first circle. When you reach the center, stitch a straight line out of the center to what will be the center of the next circle.*

STEP 3. *From that point, swirl out and stitch another circle the size of your choice.*

STEP 4. *From the end of the second circle, stitch a straight line and create another circle. Continue to stitch circles, alternating their sizes, to evenly cover the top.*

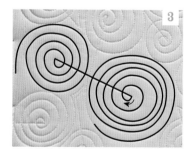

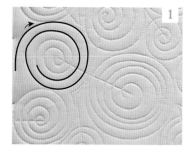
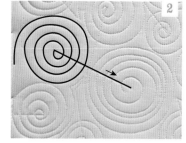

Background
FILLERS

Background fillers—similar to allover designs—can be quilted around the main motifs or blocks on the quilt top. Dense background quilting can really make the quilt motifs "pop" and add a lot of dimension. You'll find instructions here for quilting eight different designs.

PEBBLES

Pebbles should vary in size, generally between ¼˝ and ½˝, depending on the scale of the quilt. In this section, you'll learn how to stitch three different variations—single, double, and C pebbles.

Single Pebbles

Pattern is on page 167.

Stitching this simple design is an easy way to add a lot of interest to a background area.

STEP 1. *Begin stitching near a corner or side of the area you are filling. Stitch a small circle.*

STEP 2. *When you arrive back at the original starting point, stitch back on the original line to a place where you can start another pebble. Stitch a second pebble. Continue stitching adjacent pebbles until you have covered the entire area. If you come to a point where you are stuck, stitch on previous lines to get off that point.*

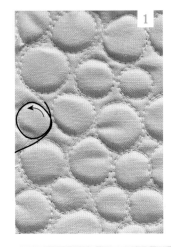
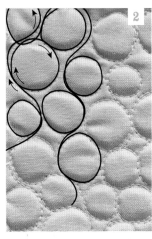

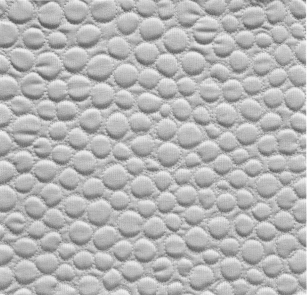

Double Pebbles

Pattern is on page 168.

Double pebbles give you a different, more complex look than single ones.

STEP 1. *Begin stitching near a corner or side of the area you are filling. Stitch a small circle. When you arrive back at the original starting point, stitch a second smaller pebble inside the first pebble.*

STEP 2. *Stitch back on the original line to a place where you can start another pebble. Stitch a second, larger pebble with another pebble inside.*

STEP 3. *Continue stitching pebbles, with smaller inner pebbles, going in opposite directions until you have covered the entire area.*

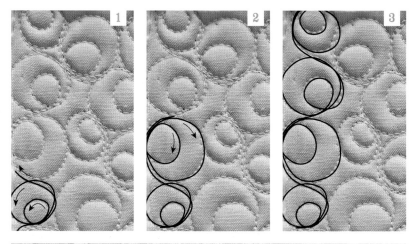

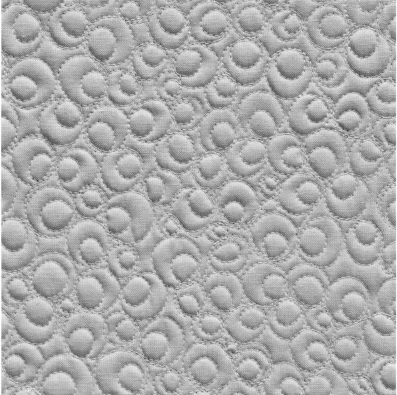

C Pebbles

Pattern is on page 169.

You get a lot of great texture with the C pebble design.

STEP 1. *Begin stitching near a corner or side of the area you are filling. Stitch a small circle. When you arrive back at the original starting point, stitch a small C shape inside the original pebble. When the C is complete, stitch back on the C stitching to the circle.*

STEP 2. *Stitch back on the original line to a place where you can start another pebble. Stitch a second larger pebble with another C shape inside. Continue stitching pebbles, with smaller inner C's, until you have covered the entire area.*

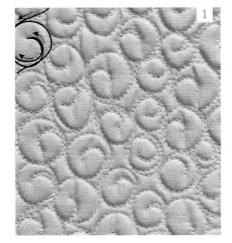

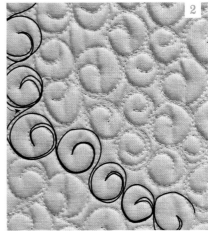

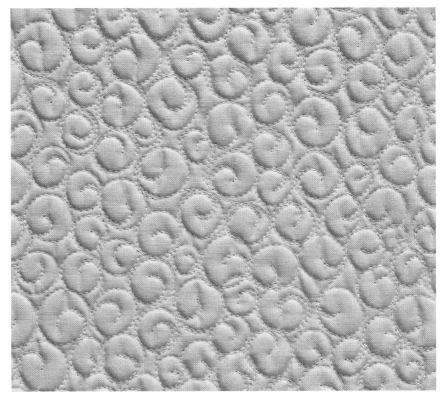

COBBLESTONES

Pattern is on page 170.

Inspired by the patterns of old-fashioned cobblestone pavings, this design looks best when you stitch cobblestones in varying sizes and in rectangular or square shapes.

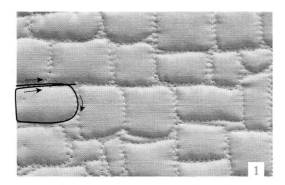

STEP 1. *Begin stitching near a corner or side of the area you are filling. Stitch a small square or rectangular cobblestone.*

STEP 2. *Stitch back on the original line to a place where you can start another cobblestone. Stitch a second larger cobblestone.*

STEP 3. *Continue stitching various sized square and rectangular cobblestones to cover the entire area.*

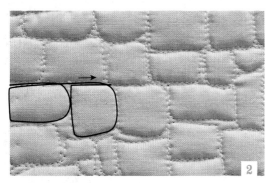

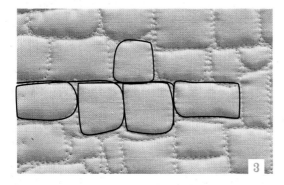

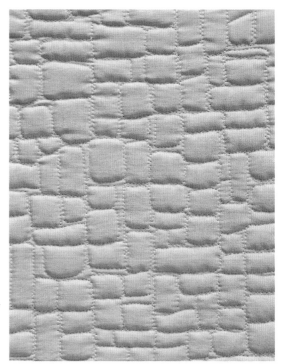

WOOD GRAIN

Pattern is on page 171.

This design is somewhat similar to Flames (page 42), but the wavy shapes are narrower and more densely packed.

STEP 1. *Begin stitching near an edge or side of the area you are filling. Stitch a small wavy line up to a point.*

STEP 2. *From the end point, stitch another wavy line, parallel to the first, back in the opposite direction. The wood grain lengths will vary in size. Stitch the wavy wood grain lines in different lengths to fill in next to other lines.*

STEP 3. *Continue stitching closely packed motifs until you have covered the entire area in a wood-grain pattern.*

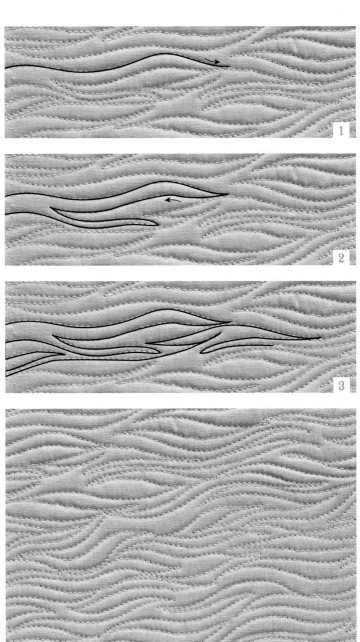

CLAMS

Pattern is on page 172.

Unlike the scalloped half-circles of the traditional clamshell pattern, these closely packed ovals really do resemble a cluster of clams!

STEP 1. *Begin stitching near an edge or side of the area you are filling. Stitch a small, elongated oval to suggest a clam shape.*

STEP 2. *Stitch an "echo" of the clam shape.*

STEP 3. *Stitch a second "echo"; then stitch a second clam going in a different direction. The second clam is done in the same manner, starting with the smallest clam first and then filling in with larger clams.*

STEP 4. *Continue stitching clam shapes with 2 or 3 echoes on each clam, varying their direction. Fill in with more clams and echoes.*

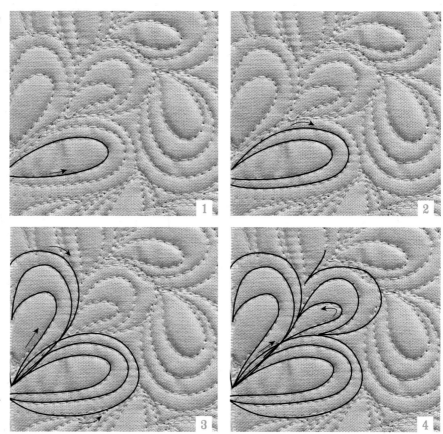

tip When you finish the second clam, you may need to move to a new space away from the first two clams to start a third clam. When this is necessary, simply stitch along a previous quilting line and then begin the next clam.

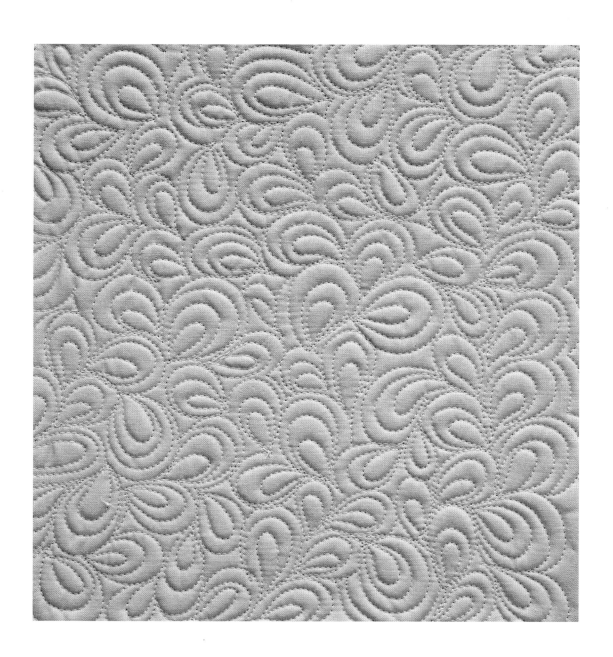

SWIRLS

Pattern is on page 173.

This design is like the swirls for allover quilting (page 34), except that these swirls are smaller and denser.

STEP 1. *Begin stitching near an edge or side of the area you are filling. Stitch in a swirl motion toward the center, leaving approximately ¼˝ between stitch lines.*

STEP 2. *When you reach the center, stop and stitch back in a swirl motion, parallel to the first line of stitching and about ⅛˝ apart.*

STEP 3. *Stitch a second swirl next to the first, turning in the opposite direction, and then stitch a parallel line back.*

STEP 4. *After completing a couple of swirls, begin stitching swirls that fill in. Stitch around the swirl and create a point to fill in between 2 swirls. Continue to stitch and fill until you have covered the entire area.*

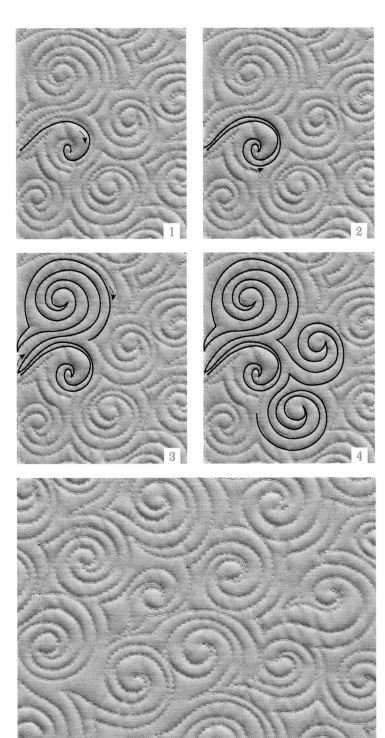

MICROSTIPPLE

Pattern is on page 174.

Stippling means stitching continuous curving lines that never cross.
Done on a small scale, it creates a very dense texture.

STEP 1. *Start stitching at an edge or side of the area you are filling. Stitch in a continuous line to create very small, wavy S shapes.*

STEP 2. *Continue the microstippling, making the shapes as small and as densely packed as desired.*

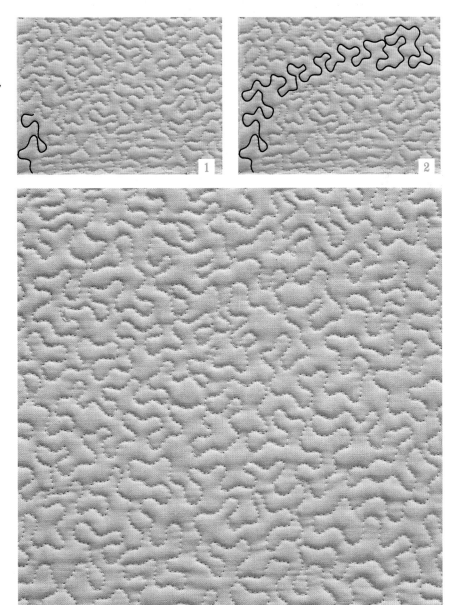

Borders and SASHINGS

Quilting in borders and sashings is a form of custom quilting tailored to those narrow strips. In this section, you'll learn how to stitch twenty designs—plenty of choices for any quilt style.

Not all patterns will fill in border corners nicely like feathers do. When quilting patterns such as hearts or figure 8's, an alternate solution is to quilt on the border edge, straight to the end of the pieced section, and then stop. Begin the next border at the edge and quilt to the opposite edge. On the next border, start again where the next pieced section starts. Continue in this manner to complete all the borders. Also, when quilting a cornerstone-pieced quilt, you will most likely want to quilt something different in the cornerstone.

FEATHERS

If you are quilting a directional feather, the feathers should go clockwise around the quilt. In these pages, you'll find instructions for quilting seven feather variations. For all of them, you will begin by quilting a single line for each feather's "spine" along the center of the border. Make this line gently curving because these feathers are intended to be soft and flowing, not stiff.

Rounded Feathers

Pattern is on page 140.

These classic feathers are a lot like the feathers for allover quilting (page 40), except they fill narrow border areas instead of meandering over the quilt top.

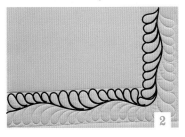

STEP 1. *Begin by stitching a spine through the center of the border. Make the vine a little curvy to give your feathers a bit of character. To stitch the first feather, begin at the bottommost point on the line you stitched for the feather spine. Stitch a single, rounded feather shape all the way to the border edge, returning to the original starting point.*

STEP 2. *Continue stitching feathers all along one side of the spine, building on top of each other and varying their size so that the rounded ends meet the border edge.*

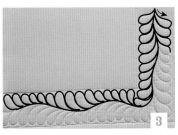

STEP 3. *After one side is complete, move onto the second side of the spine. Repeat the process, stitching feathers to fill the border entirely.*

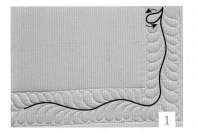

tip To create feathers on the outside of a border corner, stitch feathers as you did along the rest of the border, but this time make the feathers in the corner a little larger to fill in the extra space.

tip To create feathers on the inside of a border corner, quilt the feathers right up to one or two feathers' distance from the turn in the spine. At that point, start to stitch feathers facing in the turn direction. The first couple feathers may be a bit smaller, but they will gradually come out of the corner and be about the size of the original feathers.

Pointed Feathers

Pattern is on page 141.

Pointed feather shapes create a very different effect than rounded ones.

STEP 1. *Stitch a wavy line for the spine, as described in Rounded Feathers (page 57). To stitch the first feather, begin at the bottommost point on the line you stitched for the feather spine. Stitch an elongated S curve all the way to the border edge. Stitch back to the original starting point, creating a single narrow, pointed feather shape.*

STEP 2. *Continue stitching feathers all along one side of the spine, building on top of each other and varying their size so that the pointed ends meet the border edge. After one side is complete, move onto the second side of the spine. Repeat the process, stitching feathers to fill the border entirely.*

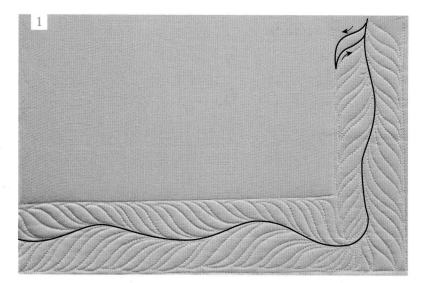

Double Feathers

Pattern is on page 142.

Add extra lines of stitching to rounded feathers to give them a different look.
This technique can be used with any type of feathers.

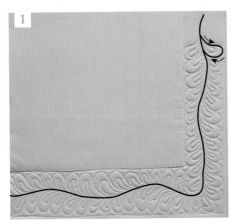

STEP 1. *Stitch a wavy line for the spine, as described in Rounded Feathers (page 57). To stitch the first feather, begin at the bottommost point on the line that you stitched for the feather spine. Stitch a single, rounded feather shape all the way to the border edge, returning to the original starting point.*

STEP 2. *At the original feather starting point, stitch a second, smaller feather inside the first one.*

STEP 3. *Continue stitching feathers all along one side of the spine, building on top of each other and adding a smaller feather inside each one. After one side is complete, move to the second side of the spine. Repeat the process, stitching double feathers to fill the border entirely.*

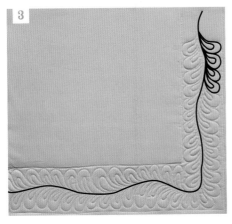

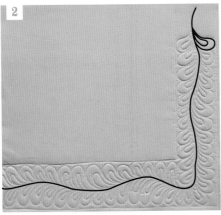

Double-Spine Feathers

Pattern is on page 143.

These feathers add a bit of a custom look with the simple addition of a second spine line stitched parallel to the first. You will quilt the same single wavy line as done in the previous feathers. This design uses the rounded feather.

STEP 1. *Stitch a wavy spine line all along the middle of the border, as described in Rounded Feathers (page 57). Then move about ¼˝ away from the original line and quilt a second, parallel spine.*

STEP 2. *Stitch the first feather, as in Rounded Feathers, stitching a single, rounded feather shape all the way to the border edge and then returning to the original starting point. Continue stitching feathers all along one side of the spine, building on top of each other and varying their size so that the rounded ends meet the border edge.*

STEP 3. *After one side is complete, move onto the second side of the spine. Repeat the process, stitching feathers to fill the border entirely.*

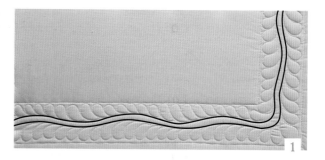

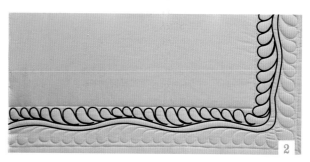

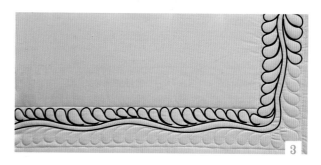

Filled-Spine Feathers

Pattern is on page 144.

Adding tiny circles inside the double spine of the feathers creates a more complex, ornate look.

STEP 1. *This design begins in the same way as described in Double-Spine Feathers (page 60, Step 1). After you complete the double spine, go back and fill it with small circles. Stitch a circle, and then stitch back along the original stitch line; stitch over to the top of what will be the second circle. Stitch the second circle and then stitch back on the original stitching line and then over to what will be the bottom of the third circle.*

STEP 2. *Repeat this process to fill the spine with circles. When all spines are filled, follow Steps 2 and 3 of Double-Spine Feathers to complete the border quilting.*

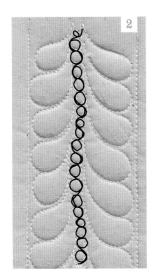

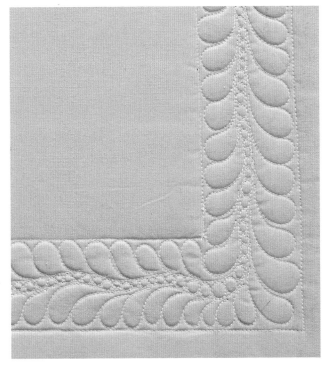

Swirl Feathers

Pattern is on page 145.

Add a swirl inside each rounded feather for a fun variation.

STEP 1. *Stitch a wavy line for the spine, as described in Rounded Feathers (page 57). To stitch the first feather, begin at the bottommost point on the line you stitched for the feather spine. Stitch a single, rounded feather shape all the way to the border edge, returning to the original starting point.*

STEP 2. *Stitch a small swirl and stitch back on the same swirl line to the original feather starting point.*

STEP 3. *Continue stitching feathers all along one side of the spine, building on top of each other and adding a small swirl inside each one. After one side is complete, move onto the second side of the spine. Repeat the process, stitching swirl feathers to fill the border entirely.*

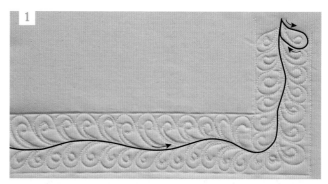

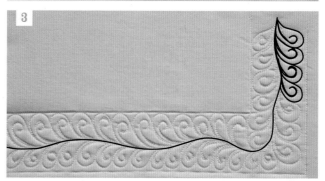

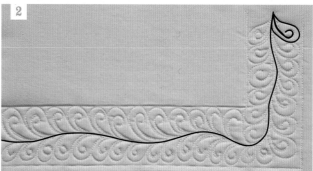

Echoed Feathers

Pattern is on page 146.

Echoing the outer line of completed feathers is simple to do but can add an interesting detailed look. You can use this with any feather design. Just be sure that you have left enough room on the outside of the feathers to add the extra stitching.

STEP 1. *Stitch the feathers as in Rounded Feathers (page 57), but be sure to end each feather at least ½˝ away from the border edge. After you finish stitching your feathers, move about ¼˝ away from the outside edges of the feathers and stitch an "echo" line all the way along.*

STEP 2. *When you have finished one side, repeat stitching the feathers and adding an echo line all along the other side. If you leave enough space beyond the edges of the feathers, you can add multiple echoes.*

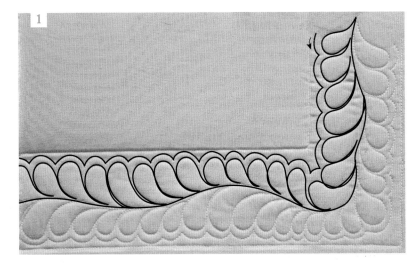

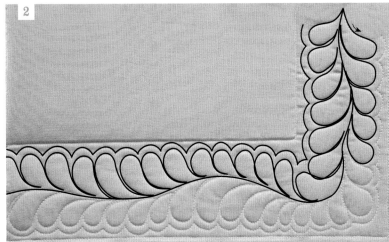

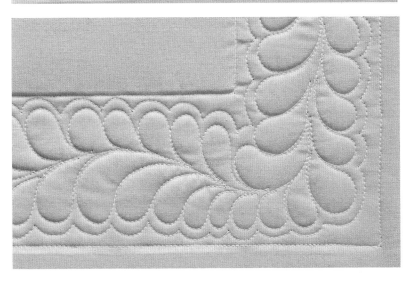

CIRCLES

Circles are a very simple way to add detail to a border. In this section, you will learn to make three variations: single circles, double circles, and triple circles.

Single Circles

Pattern is on page 147.

These are so simple to stitch!

STEP 1. *Begin stitching on the inside of the border, starting near a corner so the corners will turn out right. Stitch a single circle, coming back to the original starting point.*

STEP 2. *Stitch away from that circle to the opposite side of the border, and create another circle.*

STEP 3. *Repeat Steps 1 and 2, creating circles in opposite directions all the way around the quilt border.*

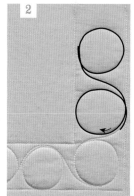
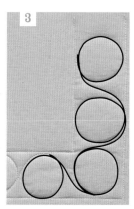

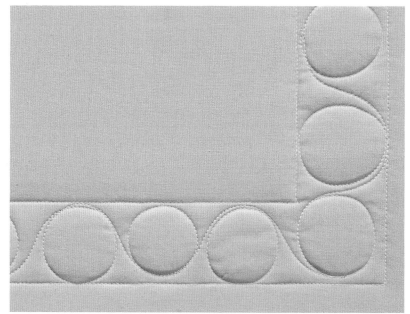

tip As you approach each border corner, judge the distance that you will need to make a circle end up in the corner. Lengthen or shorten the space between the circles before the corner so the corner circle will fall exactly in the right space. In the beginning, you may want to sketch your quilting pattern on your quilt to ensure that the circles end up in the corners.

Double Circles

Pattern is on page 148.

Build on the single circle to create these more detailed circles.

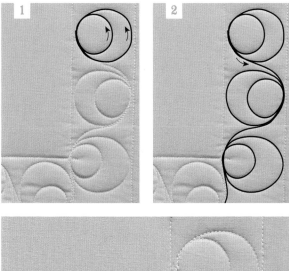

Triple Circles

Pattern is on page 149.

Here's one more variation on simple circles.

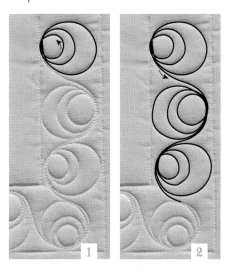

STEP 1. *Stitch a circle, as described in Single Circles. Then stitch the second circle as in Double Circles, but this time, after completing the second circle, stitch a smaller third circle inside.*

STEP 2. *Repeat this process all the way around the quilt border.*

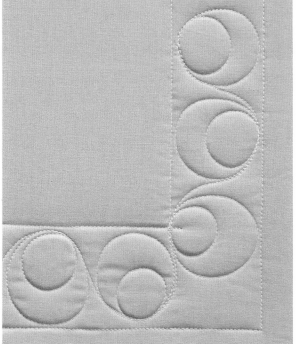

STEP 1. *Stitch a circle, as described in Single Circles. Stop at the original starting point, and stitch a smaller second circle inside.*

STEP 2. *Repeat this process all the way around the quilt border.*

SWIRLS

Pattern is on page 150.

Swirls are such a versatile design; they work just as well in borders as they do in allover quilting.

STEP 1. *Choose a starting point near the border's inner edge. Stitch toward the outside of the border and then create a swirl, as described in allover quilting Swirls (page 34).*

STEP 2. *Stitch back out on the same swirl line. Stop near the border's outer edge, and stitch another swirl going in the opposite direction.*

STEP 3. *Continue stitching swirls in alternate directions all the way around the quilt border.*

tip Swirls are pretty forgiving when it comes to corners. When you get close to a corner, you will want to start judging the distance that you will need to make a swirl end up in the corner. I like to make the swirl right before the corner to end near the point where the borders meet.

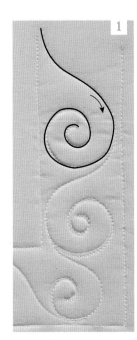

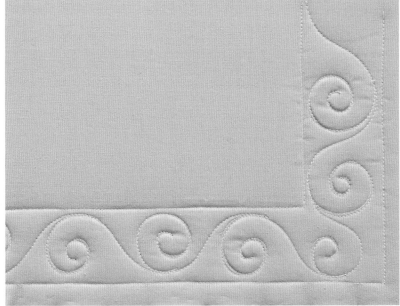

OVALS

Pattern is on page 151.

Ovals look interesting because of their shape and the looped connections stitched between them.

STEP 1. *Decide if you want the rounded ends of the ovals to point toward the center of the quilt or toward the outer edge, as shown here. Start stitching on the side opposite from the way you want them to point. For example, to make them point toward the outer edge, start stitching on the inside as shown. If you'd like them to point toward the center, start stitching on the outside. Stitch a single oval and come back to the original starting point.*

STEP 2. *Loop up past the starting point and stitch a second oval in the same direction, right next to the first one. Repeat Steps 1 and 2 until you have multiple ovals, all pointing in the same direction all the way around the quilt border.*

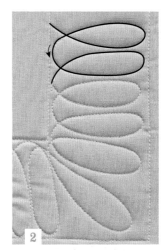

tip When you get to the corner, you have two options: You can run the ovals straight to the end of the border, or you can stitch the ovals into the corner. To stitch the ovals into the corner, continue stitching the ovals until you are just about to the inside point of the corner. When you get to that point, start stitching the ovals in more of an angle, making one oval point right into the corner. That corner oval will be longer than the others.

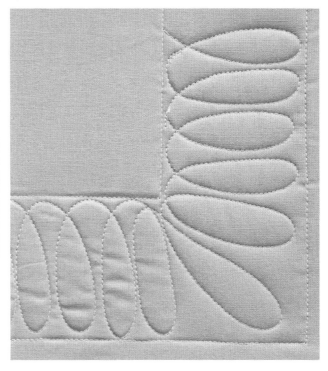

FLOWERS

Flowers are simple to quilt and can add a lot of fun and frill to a border. In this section, you will learn to make two variations: daisies and poppies.

Daisies

Pattern is on page 152.

The daisy is a design that works for a border, as well as for all-over quilting.

STEP 1. *To create a daisy, start in the center of the border and stitch a curved line out to a point at the border's inner edge, where you want the petal to end.*

STEP 2. *Stitch a curved line that mirrors the first, continuing back to the center to complete one petal.*

STEP 3. *Repeat Steps 1 and 2 to make 5 daisy petals in a circle. (The inner ends will not meet.) When you get back to the center of the fifth petal, stitch a small circle in the middle.*

STEP 4. *Stitch a wavy line to what will be the center of the next daisy. Repeat the entire process to make a continuous chain of daisies all the way around the quilt border.*

tip When you come to the corner, you may need to stitch the flower that will fit in the corner a little bit farther from the previous flower so that you will have one right in the corner.

Poppies

Pattern is on page 153.

Poppies are essentially done the same way as daisies, but their petals are more rounded.

STEP 1. *To create a poppy, start in the center of the border and stitch a rounded petal.*

STEP 2. *Repeat Step 1 to stitch 5 petals in a circle.*

STEP 3. *When you get back to the center of the fifth petal, stitch a small circle in the middle. Stitch a wavy line to what will be the center of the next poppy.*

STEP 4. *Repeat Steps 1–3 to make a continuous chain of poppies all the way around the quilt border. The border corners are made the same way as described in Daisies (page 68).*

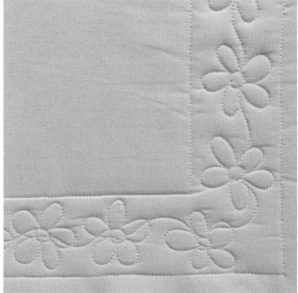

Echoed Daisies and Echoed Poppies

Pattern for Echoed Daisies is on page 154.

If you'd like a little bit heavier quilting, you can add echoing to basic daisies and poppies.

STEP 1. *Follow the instructions for Daisies (page 68) or Poppies (page 70) to stitch all the flowers in the border. The petals of the flowers should not go any closer than ½˝ to the border's edges, so there will be room for the echo lines.*

STEP 2. *Beginning about ¼˝ from the flower petals, stitch an outline, or echo, around the pattern, stitching around the flowers and connecting vines all the way around the quilt border. You can add a second echo, as shown here, if there is space.*

For a more custom look, try stitching multiple echoing. When stitching the original flower shapes, be sure to leave enough room for the echo stitching lines.

tip Even though the poppy did not fall exactly in the corner in the example shown, it looks okay because the chain between the flowers falls in the corner. You can plan the corners however you like, but try to make all four corners consistent. Alternatively, you can match opposite pairs of corners, so that you end up with two different corner styles for the quilt.

LEAVES

Pattern is on page 155.

Leaves lend a touch of nature to the borders.

STEP 1. *Begin stitching at the inner part of the border. Stitch up the center to create a vein. Stop and come back down the vein to the base of the leaf.*

STEP 2. *Stitch a gently curving line around one side to just above the top of the vein; then stitch a mirror line back down the opposite side to the base.*

STEP 3. *Stitch a curved line back to the opposite side of the border to the point where you will start another leaf.*

STEP 4. *Repeat Steps 1–3, stitching leaves in opposite directions all the way around the quilt border.*

tip As you approach the border corner, judge the distance that you will need to make one leaf fit right into the corner. Sometimes you may have to make some of the leaves before the corner a little larger or smaller to accommodate the corner leaf.

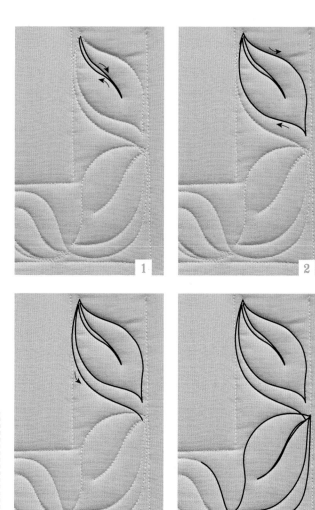

HEARTS

Pattern is on page 156.

This design adds a sweet touch to the borders.

STEP 1. *Starting at a point just inside the border's inner edge, stitch a half-heart out to the border's outer edge.*

STEP 2. *When you are near the bottom of the heart, turn and stitch another half-heart in the opposite direction.*

STEP 3. *From the center point, stitch the second half of the heart and loop around at the border's inner edge to create the top half of the next heart.*

STEP 4. *Repeat Steps 1–3 to stitch hearts all the way around the quilt border.*

tip To create the best-looking corners, space the hearts so you can stitch one heart facing at an angle in the corner. Or it may be easiest to stitch the hearts straight to the end of the border and then start again at the next border's edge, as shown here.

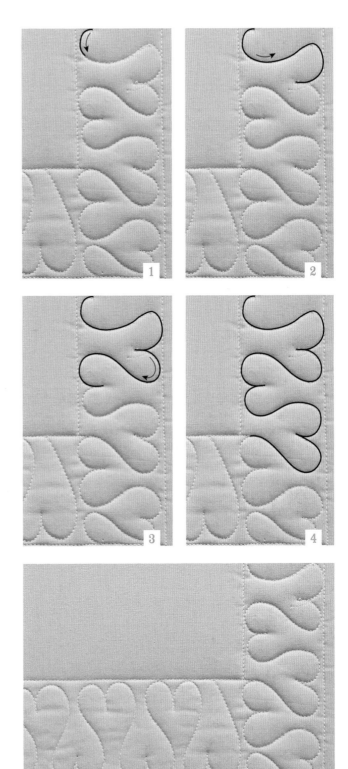

FIGURE 8'S

Pattern is on page 157.

This one is fun to stitch!

STEP 1. *Begin stitching at a point in the center of the border; stitch to the opposite side of the border and create a loop on the border's outside edge.*

STEP 2. *Stitch back to the opposite side, creating a figure 8. Make the loops as large or as small as you'd like—for a lacier look, make the loops smaller (about ¼˝ wide); for a more playful look, make the loops larger (about ½˝ wide).*

STEP 3. *Repeat this process to stitch multiple figure 8's side by side, all around the quilt border.*

tip For the best result when quilting figure 8's into corners, I suggest quilting straight to the end of the border. Then start again in the border that is going in the other direction.

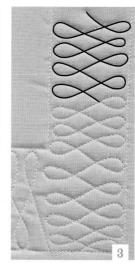
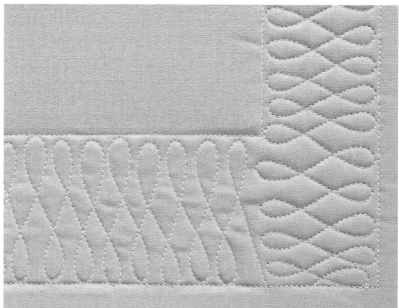

S'S

Pattern is on page 158.

These S's wind up looking a lot like pointed feathers (page 58).

STEP 1. *Begin stitching at a point on the inner edge of the border. Stitch an elongated S shape toward the opposite side of the border.*

STEP 2. *Stitch back to the opposite side of the border with another S shape.*

STEP 3. *Repeat Steps 1 and 2 to stitch S shapes all the way around the quilt border.*

tip When you come to the corner, you will want to fill on a curve. Stitch the S's a little bit larger to nicely fit into the corner. You also may need to fill with a few smaller S shapes as you turn the corner.

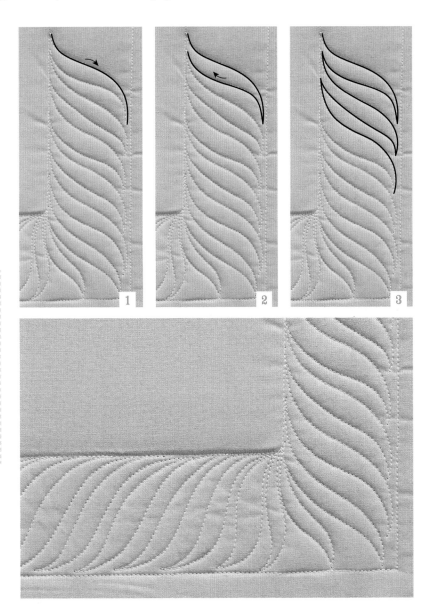

Custom Quilted BLOCKS

You can use custom quilting—quilting that is designed to fill a special area—to add extra dimension to the blocks. The quilting design can be done on pieced blocks, like feathers, arcs, and swirls in a Nine-Patch block. Or you can dress up plain blocks with flowers, letters, and other designs. In this section, you'll learn to quilt eight different designs and variations.

FEATHERS

A ring of feathers looks beautiful on any block, plain or pieced. The feathers can either fill the block by making larger feathers at the block's corners or form a perfect circle of equal-sized feathers.

For a circle of feathers, first draw the center circle on the quilt. Use a blue water-soluble pen to draw around an object of appropriate size, such as a CD, a plate, or even a spool of thread. If the fabric is dark, use white or light-colored chalk. You can stitch single or double feathers.

If you want a perfectly round medallion feather, you will need to keep the outer part of the feather consistent. Draw a second, larger circle, and then stitch the feathers out to that larger circle.

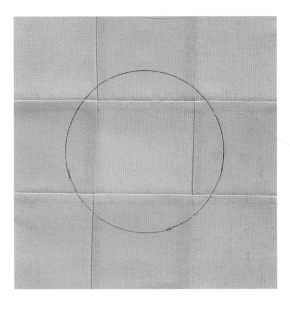

> *tip* I prefer to quilt the feathers right out to the edge of the quilt block. If I do leave a small space unquilted, I generally don't like to leave it bigger than about ⅛˝. If you are quilting a round feather medallion in a square block, make the corner feathers larger than the feathers on the sides.

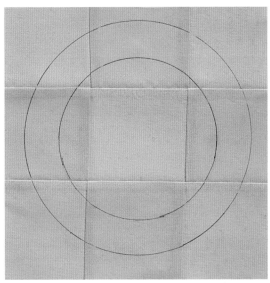

Single Feathers

Pattern is on page 159.

For additional basic information on quilting this design, see the instructions in Allover Quilting for Feathers (page 40).

STEP 1. *After you have drawn the circle, choose a starting point on the outside of the circle; begin stitching at the base of one feather. Stitch feathers one at a time, close together, around the circle.*

STEP 2. *Complete the entire outer ring of feathers.*

STEP 3. *After the outer feathers are complete, stitch on the original marked line.*

STEP 4. *Stitch smaller feathers all around the inside of the circle. After quilting is complete, spray the marked line with water, and it will disappear.*

Double Feathers

Pattern is on page 160.

These are a little bit more detailed than the single feathers (page 78).

STEP 1. *After you have drawn the circle, choose a starting point on the outside of the circle, and begin stitching at the base of one feather. Stitch a complete feather.*

STEP 2. *Stitch back to the starting point, and stitch a smaller feather inside the original feather.*

STEP 3. *Repeat Steps 1 and 2 to stitch all the double feathers on the outside of the circle.*

STEP 4. *After the outer feathers are complete, stitch on the original marked line, to add smaller feathers around the inside of the circle, sewing an even smaller feather inside each one. After quilting is complete, spray the marked line with water, and it will disappear.*

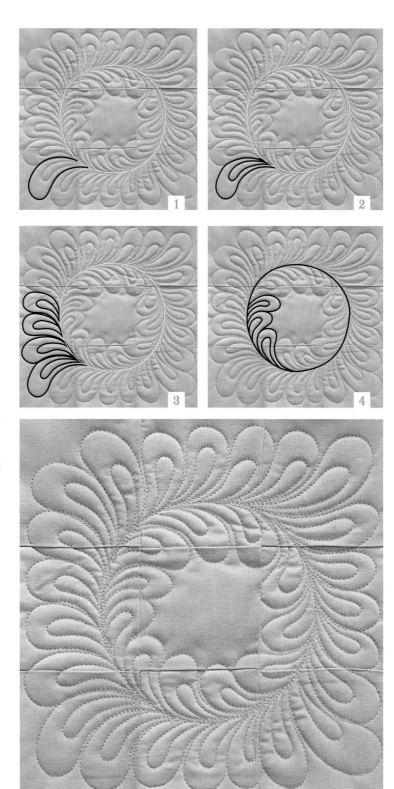

ARCS

Arcs are very simple and can be used to highlight elements in a block, as in this Nine-Patch. In this section, you will learn to make two variations: single arcs and double arcs.

Single Arcs

Pattern is on page 61.

This is the simplest of designs; here it is quilted on a Nine-Patch block.

STEP 1. *Begin in one corner of a block unit and stitch an arc to the next corner within the unit/patch.*

STEP 2. *Repeat Step 1 on all 4 sides of the unit if you are doing just one patch.*

STEP 3. *If you are quilting multiple block units with arcs side by side, start quilting on the upper right corner block unit and stitch the arcs on 3 sides of this first block unit.*

STEP 4. *Move to the next block unit and repeat Step 3, stitching arcs on 3 sides.*

STEP 5. *Repeat the entire process to stitch arcs on all the block units. When you reach a point where you are ready to come back, stitch the fourth arc on multiple units.*

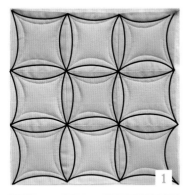

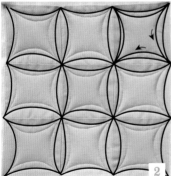

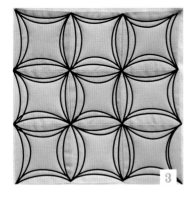

Double Arcs

Pattern is on page 162.

Double arcs add a little extra to the basic arc design.

STEP 1. *Stitch a complete first set of arcs, as described in Single Arcs (page 80).*

STEP 2. *Go back through in the reverse order you stitched the first arcs, and stitch a second, larger arc.*

STEP 3. *Repeat Steps 1 and 2 to create a complete set of double arcs.*

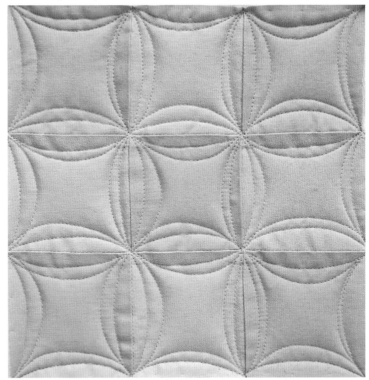

SWIRLS

Pattern is on page 163.

Swirls stitched in each unit of a Nine-Patch block make an interesting overall pattern when they are all oriented as shown in this sequence.

STEP 1. *Begin in one corner of a block unit and stitch a swirl.*

STEP 2. *Swirl back out to the opposite corner. From this point, you can stop or you can move on to another block unit and continue creating multiple swirl units, orienting the swirls in alternating directions.*

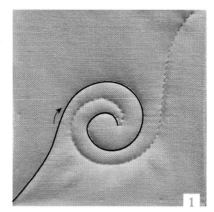
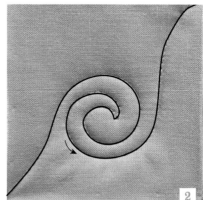

MOTIFS IN PLAIN BLOCKS

Dress up plain blocks with large single motifs that take center stage.

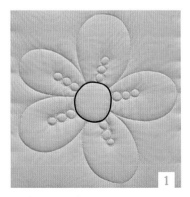

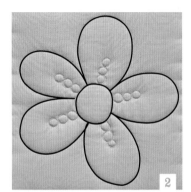

Flower

Pattern is on page 164.

This flower has special decorative designs on each petal.

STEP 1. *In the center of the block, stitch a small circle for the flower center.*

STEP 2. *Stitch 5 rounded petals of equal size around the center, bringing each petal almost to the edge of the block.*

STEP 3. *When you arrive back at the center, stitch to the center of each flower petal; then stitch 3 small circles (page 88) up the center of the flower. Repeat this step for all 5 petals.*

Vine

Pattern is on page 165.

A simple, swirled vine is easy to do and adds a nice touch.

STEP 1. *Starting at one corner of the block, stitch a swirling line into the center.*

STEP 2. *Stitch the swirl back out to the corner. Repeat this process on just one or multiple corners to achieve the desired look.*

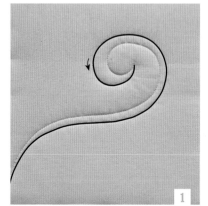

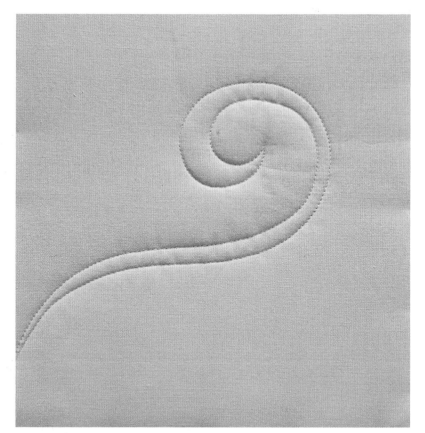

Letter

To add the letter of your choice, go to a printing program on your computer, choose the font and size that is appropriate for the block, and print the letter on regular paper.

STEP 1. *Use a blue water-soluble pen to trace the letter onto the block.*

STEP 2. *Stitch on the marked line. After quilting, spray with water to remove the blue ink.*

tip When you stop and start, make sure to take a few securing stitches because there could be quite a few stops and starts when quilting letters.

Quilting on APPLIQUÉ

Custom quilting can really make your appliqué blocks pop! In this section, you'll find three designs to quilt on an appliquéd flower; adapt these designs to leaves and other appliqués.

87 **VEINS**   88 **CIRCLES**   89 **SWIRLED CENTER**

VEINS

Flowers and leaves can be enhanced by quilting small veins on them.

STEP 1. *Start stitching at the base of the flower petal or leaf, and stitch a wavy line up and then back down over itself.*

STEP 2. *From the base, make a couple of stitches and repeat Step 1. Move to the next petal via stitches at the base around the flower center. Continue to add veins to the petals.*

tip On a small-scale flower (or leaf), a single vein may be enough. Just place the vein in the middle of the petal (see *Daisy Drops,* page 110).

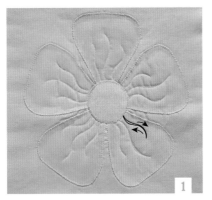

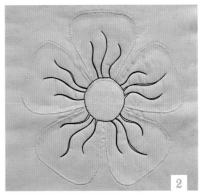

CIRCLES

A string of little circles on the petal adds a cute touch. For more details on stitching these, refer to Step 3 of Flower (page 83).

STEP 1. *Begin stitching at the base of the petal. Stitch 3 or 4 small circles up the center of the petal.*

STEP 2. *Stitch back to the petal of the flower on the original stitching lines; then stitch around the center circle to the next petal to make the circles there. Repeat for the remaining petals.*

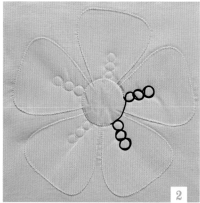

SWIRLED CENTER

Swirls work well on circles or flower centers. To dress up the flower petals, simply stitch echoing lines around them. Start with a flower on which you have already stitched veins (see page 87).

STEP 1. *For the center, start stitching on the outside of the circle, and swirl to the inside. Swirl back out on the same line to the original starting point.*

STEP 2. *Stitch a small echo line around each petal, about ¼˝ from the outside of the appliqué. You can do this with any appliqué shape. If the appliqué is large, you can stitch multiple echoing, or stitch ½˝ from the outer appliqué line.*

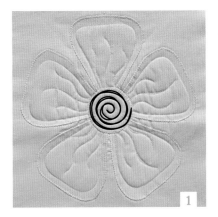

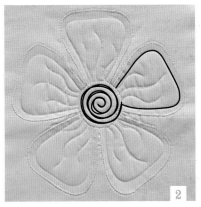

SIX QUILT PROJECTS TO MAKE

Now that you've developed quilting skills, why not make a fresh new quilt to show them off? In this section, you'll find six simple projects that use piecing and appliqué. When you've assembled your chosen quilt top, turn to any of the quilting tutorials and patterns to give it that special finishing touch. For each project, I've included suggested quilting designs.

Finished size: 84˝ × 84˝

AMAZED

Designed, made, and quilted by Natalia Bonner, and bound by Kathleen Whiting

This quilt is made with two different blocks—one appliquéd and one pieced. It uses just three fabrics; the darker-value pink and gray really stand out on a simple white background, and the small-scale dot print lets the bold shapes play the starring role.

MATERIALS

Yardages are based on fabric that is at least 40˝ wide.

5 yards of white fabric

1⅔ yards of pink fabric

2⅜ yards of gray fabric

¾ yards of binding fabric

7¾ yards of backing fabric

2⅝ yards of 96˝-wide batting

CUTTING

Before cutting out the pieces to be appliquéd, refer to Appliqué Method (page 95).

White:

Cut 140 squares 2˝ × 2˝.

Cut 35 squares 3½˝ × 3½˝.

Cut 28 rectangles 2˝ × 12½˝.

Cut 14 rectangles 6½˝ × 12½˝.

Cut 140 rectangles 3½˝ × 6½˝.

Pink:

Cut 280 squares 2˝ × 2˝.

Cut 140 rectangles 2˝ × 3½˝.

Cut 1 strip 9˝ × WOF (width of fabric), starch, and then cut into 12 squares 4˝ × 4˝ for appliqué squares.

Gray:

Cut 210 squares 2˝ × 2˝.

Cut 70 rectangles 2˝ × 3½˝.

Cut 70 rectangles 2˝ × 5˝.

Cut 28 rectangles 2˝ × 12˝.

MAKING THE BLOCKS

Seam allowances are ¼˝ unless otherwise indicated.

This quilt has two blocks: Block 1 is pieced and appliquéd, and Block 2 is pieced.

Block 1

1. Sew a 2˝ × 12½˝ gray rectangle and a 2˝ × 12½˝ white rectangle together along the long sides (Figure 1). Press.

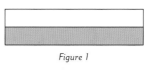

Figure 1

2. Sew the gray/white strip set from Step 1 to each side of a 6½˝ × 12½˝ white rectangle.

3. Repeat Steps 1 and 2 to make a total of 14 Block 1's (Figure 2). Press.

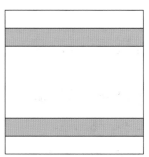

Figure 2

4. Refer to Appliqué Method (page 95) to prepare and randomly appliqué a 4˝ × 4˝ pink square onto each of 12 Block 1's (Figure 3). Refer to the quilt assembly diagram (page 96) for appliqué placement.

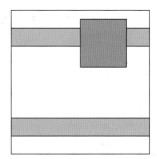

Figure 3

Block 2

1. Sew 2 pink 2˝ × 3½˝ rectangles to opposite sides of a white 3½˝ × 3½˝ square. Press. Make 35 pink/white units.

2. Sew a pink 2˝ × 2˝ square to the end of a gray 2˝ × 5˝ rectangle. Press. Make 70 pink/gray units.

3. Sew a pink/gray unit to each side of the pink/white unit made in Step 1 (Figure 4). Make 35 square center units.

4. Sew 2 pink 2˝ × 2˝ squares onto 2 adjacent corners of each 3½˝ × 6½˝ white rectangle by placing a square on a rectangle corner, right sides together, and sewing a diagonal seam from corner to corner of the square. Trim seams and press open (Figure 5). Make 70 pink/white rectangle units.

5. In the same manner as in Step 4, sew 2 gray 2˝ × 2˝ squares onto the adjacent corners of a 3½˝ × 6½˝ white rectangle by placing a square on a rectangle corner, right sides together, and sewing a diagonal seam from corner to corner of the square. Trim seams and press open (Figure 6). Make 70 gray/white rectangle units.

6. Sew a white 2˝ × 2˝ square to a gray 2˝ × 2˝ square to make 70 gray/white units total, and sew a white 2˝ × 2˝ square to a pink 2˝ × 2˝ square to make 70 pink/white square units total. Press.

7. Sew a pink 2˝ × 3½˝ strip to each of the gray/white square units from Step 6 (Figure 7). Press.

8. Sew a gray 2˝ × 3½˝ strip to each of the pink/white square units from Step 6 (Figure 8). Press.

9. Sew the gray/white rectangle units from Step 5 to the sides of the square center units from Step 3 (Figure 9). Press.

10. Sew a unit from Step 7 and a unit from Step 8 to the opposite ends of a pink/white rectangle unit from Step 4 (Figure 10). Press.

11. Sew the units from Step 10 to the block centers (Figure 11). Press.

12. Repeat Steps 1–11 to make a total of 35 Block 2's.

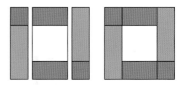

Figure 4

Trim.
Stitch.

Figure 5

Figure 6

Figure 7   *Figure 8*

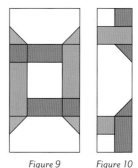

Figure 9   *Figure 10*

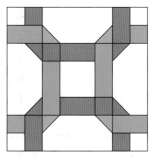

Figure 11

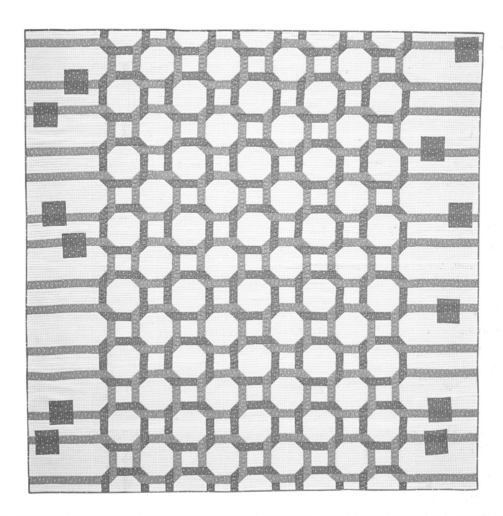

APPLIQUÉ METHOD

Before cutting out the appliqué pieces, spray the fabric with several applications of starch. After each application, press the fabric to ensure it is dry. Repeat until the fabric is stiff.

I use a raw-edge starch method to attach the appliqué pieces, instead of using fusible web. The starch method allows me to cut away the background fabric behind my appliqués after they are applied. The background fabric can often show through an appliqué, especially when the background is darker than the appliqué; cutting away the background helps prevent this show-through. Cutting away also reduces wear in heavy areas and makes for smoother machine quilting.

Cut out the shapes from the starched fabric. Use a water-soluble gluestick on the appliqué piece's edges to glue it in place. Set your machine to a blanket stitch, and stitch around the appliqué piece. There is no need to turn under the edges of the appliqué because the starch prevents fraying while stitching.

Cut out the fabric from behind the appliqué, leaving a ¼˝ seam allowance around the appliqué's edges, especially if the underneath fabric is showing through. Be very careful to cut into only the background fabric.

Wait until the quilt is quilted and bound before washing out the starch and glue.

PUTTING IT ALL TOGETHER

1. Refer to the assembly diagram to sew 2 rows of Block 1's side by side, with 7 blocks in each row. Press.

2. Sew together 5 Block 2's side by side to make a row; ensure that the pinks are sewn next to each other to achieve the woven look. Press. Make 7 Block 2 rows.

3. Sew the Block 2 rows together. Press.

4. Sew the Block 1 rows to the sides of the quilt. Press.

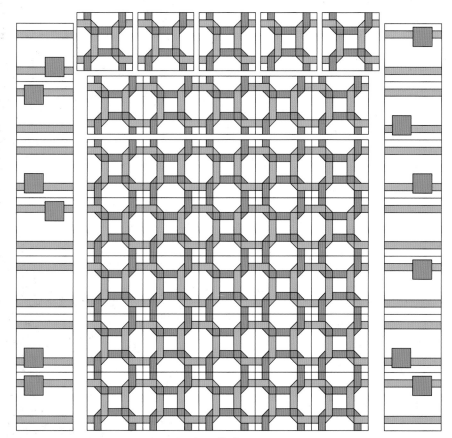

Assembly diagram

QUILTING AND FINISHING

1. Mark the quilting design on the quilt top as described in How to Use the Quilting Patterns (page 23), or plan to free-motion quilt without marking.

2. Refer to Layering and Basting (page 17) to layer and baste the quilt top, batting, and backing.

3. Quilt as desired. Good quilting designs for this quilt are border and sashing patterns, such as Ovals (page 67). For the background filler, you can sew straight lines as described in Straight-Line Quilting (page 22). I used a straight-line quilting design in the white background areas, with the lines ½˝ apart. In the gray and pink strips, I quilted ovals using a coordinating thread color. On the appliqué pieces, I stitched a square that swirled into the center, keeping stitch lines ¼˝ apart until I got to the center.

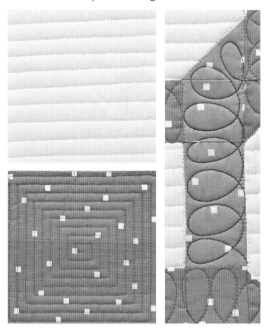

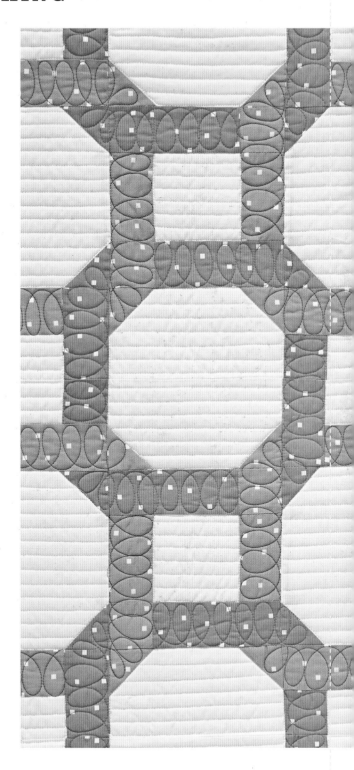

4. Refer to Binding (page 121) to bind the quilt. Then square it up as described in Squaring Up Your Quilt (page 23).

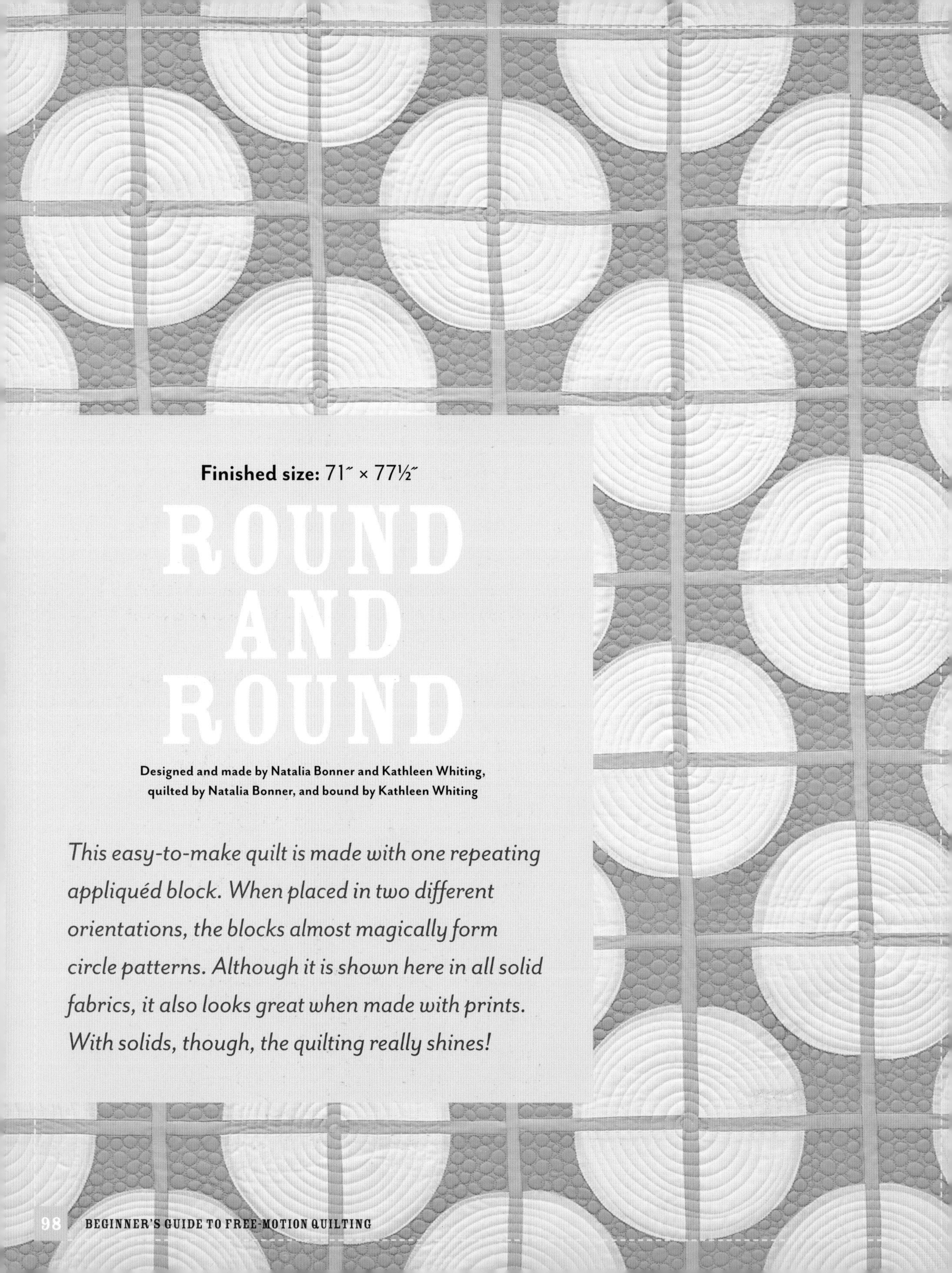

Finished size: 71˝ × 77½˝

ROUND AND ROUND

Designed and made by Natalia Bonner and Kathleen Whiting,
quilted by Natalia Bonner, and bound by Kathleen Whiting

This easy-to-make quilt is made with one repeating appliquéd block. When placed in two different orientations, the blocks almost magically form circle patterns. Although it is shown here in all solid fabrics, it also looks great when made with prints. With solids, though, the quilting really shines!

MATERIALS

Yardages are based on fabric that is at least 40˝ wide.

3¾ yards of white fabric

1¼ yards of blue fabric

4¼ yards of green fabric

¾ yard of binding fabric

4¾ yards of backing fabric

2⅜ yards of 96˝-wide batting

CUTTING

Template is on page 101. Before cutting out the pieces to be appliquéd, refer to Appliqué Method (page 95).

White:

Cut 264 pieces using template A.

Green:

Cut 132 squares 6½˝ × 6½˝.

Blue:

Cut 22 strips 1˝ × WOF (width of fabric); piece end to end as needed, and subcut into 11 strips 1˝ × 71½˝.

Cut 120 strips 1˝ × 6½˝.

MAKING THE BLOCKS

1. Prepare the white appliqué A pieces as described in Appliqué Method (page 95).

2. Use a blanket stitch or satin stitch to sew 2 white A pieces onto each of the 144 green 6½˝ × 6½˝ squares.

3. Carefully trim away the green background fabric from behind the appliqué, leaving ¼˝ seam allowance all around.

PUTTING IT ALL TOGETHER

Seam allowances are ¼˝ unless otherwise indicated.

1. Refer to the assembly diagram to sew together the blocks, placing the 1˝ × 6½˝ blue sashing strips between the blocks. Sew 12 rows of 11 blocks each, alternating the orientation of the blocks as shown to create circle patterns.

2. Sew together the 12 rows, placing the 1˝ × 71½˝ blue sashing strips between rows.

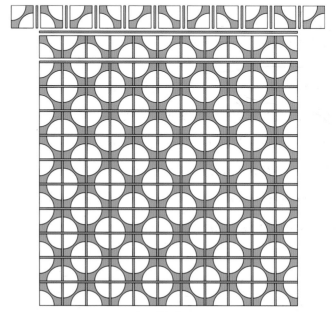

Assembly diagram

QUILTING AND FINISHING

1. Mark the quilting design on the quilt top as described in How to Use the Quilting Patterns (page 23), or plan to free-motion quilt without marking.

2. Refer to Layering and Basting (page 17) to layer and baste the quilt top, batting, and backing.

3. Quilt as desired. Good quilting designs for this quilt are Pebbles (page 47) and Swirls (page 34). I quilted large swirls in white thread on each white circle; in the green background areas, I quilted pebbles using thread in a matching green color.

4. Refer to Binding (page 121) to bind the quilt. Square it up as described in Squaring Up Your Quilt (page 23).

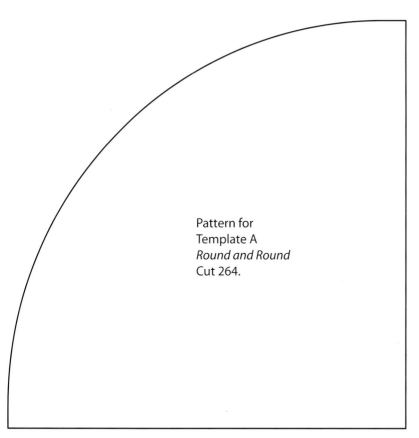

Pattern for
Template A
Round and Round
Cut 264.

Template A

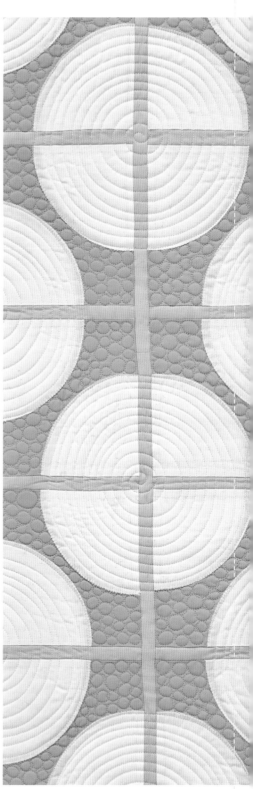

Finished size: 64˝ × 64˝

ORANGE SLICES

Designed and quilted by Natalia Bonner, made by Ilene Peterson, and bound by Kathleen Whiting

This simple appliquéd quilt is made from solid fabrics in two colors—white and, of course, orange. It's fun made as orange slices, but it would also be darling in yellow (lemons), green (limes), or pink (grapefruit)! The quilting adds lots of interest, but creating the appliqués with prints would add even more texture.

Yardages are based on fabric that is at least 40˝ wide.

4 yards of white fabric

2 yards of orange fabric

¾ yard of binding fabric

4 yards of backing fabric

2 yards of 96˝-wide batting

Iron-on transfer pen (*optional*)

CUTTING

Template is on page 105. Before cutting out the pieces to be appliquéd, refer to Appliqué Method (page 95).

White:

Cut 16 squares 16½˝ × 16½˝.

Orange:

Cut 192 pieces using template B.

MAKING THE BLOCKS

1. Prepare the Orange Slice appliqué B pieces as described in Appliqué Method (page 95).

2. Enlarge the Orange Slice placement guide (page 105) 200%. Make 4 copies of the enlarged pattern and attach together along the dotted lines to make the full circle pattern. Place the pattern on a lightbox or window. Then place each white 16½˝ × 16½˝ block over it, and trace the design with a pencil or erasable marker. This process will ensure exact placement of the orange slice appliqués. (Alternatively, you can use a transfer pencil to trace over the lines on the enlarged pattern. Press the traced pattern onto each of the 16 white 16½˝ × 16½˝ blocks to create a circle of 12 "slices.")

3. Use a blanket stitch or satin stitch to appliqué 12 orange slices onto each of the 16 blocks.

PUTTING IT ALL TOGETHER

Seam allowances are ¼˝ unless otherwise indicated.

1. Refer to the assembly diagram to sew the blocks into 4 rows of 4 blocks each. Press.

2. Sew the 4 rows together. Press.

Assembly diagram

QUILTING AND FINISHING

1. Mark the quilting design on the quilt top as described in How to Use the Quilting Patterns (page 23), or plan to free-motion quilt without marking.

2. Refer to Layering and Basting (page 17) to layer and baste the quilt top, batting, and backing.

3. Quilt as desired. Good quilting designs for this quilt are echoing and Figure 8's (page 74). I echo-quilted the background with white thread, following the curved edges of the orange "slices." On each orange appliqué, I quilted Figure 8's.

4. Refer to Binding (page 121) to bind the quilt. Square it up as described in Squaring Up Your Quilt (page 23).

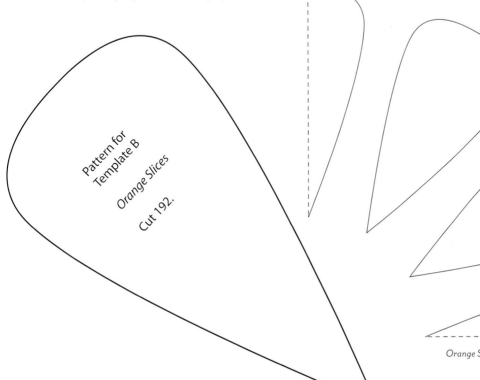

Pattern for Template B

Orange Slices

Cut 192.

Orange Slices placement guide—enlarge 200%.

Finished size: 80˝ × 80˝

TWISTED UP

Designed, made, and quilted by Natalia Bonner, and bound by Kathleen Whiting

Two tone-on-tone prints and a plain white background play up this quilt's bold design. It would be great made with any two prints and a contrasting solid. Simple piecing with strips creates the illusion of interlinked frames.

MATERIALS

Yardages are based on fabric that is at least 40˝ wide.

2⅛ yards of green fabric

2⅛ yards of purple fabric

2⅞ yards of white fabric

⅝ yard of binding fabric

7⅜ yards of backing fabric

2½ yards of 96˝-wide batting

CUTTING

WOF = width of fabric

The numbers and letters indicate section numbers and piece letters. It is a good idea to sort all the pieces by section number as you cut them out.

Green:

Cut 8 strips 2½˝ × WOF; subcut into 64 strips 2½˝ × 4½˝ (1B, 2B, 3B, 4B).

Cut 8 strips 2½˝ × WOF; subcut into 32 strips 2½˝ × 8½˝ (1D, 2D).

Cut 8 strips 2½˝ × WOF; subcut into 32 strips 2½˝ × 10½˝ (3H, 4H).

From the leftover ends of these strips, cut 32 squares 2½˝ × 2½˝ (2F, 4F).

Purple:

Cut 8 strips 2½˝ × WOF; subcut into 64 squares 2½˝ × 4½˝ (1C, 2C, 3C, 4C).

Cut 8 strips 2½˝ × WOF; subcut into 32 strips 2½˝ × 8½˝ (3D, 4D).

Cut 11 strips 2½˝ × WOF; subcut into 32 strips 2½˝ × 10½˝ (1H, 2H).

From the leftover ends of these strips, cut 32 squares 2½˝ × 2½˝ (1F, 3F).

White:

Cut 8 strips 4½˝ × WOF; subcut into 64 squares 4½˝ × 4½˝ (1A, 2A, 3A, 4A).

Cut 16 strips 2½˝ × WOF; subcut into 96 strips 2½˝ × 6½˝ (1E, 2E, 3E, 4E, 2I, 3I).

Cut 8 strips 2½˝ × WOF; subcut into 32 strips 2½˝ × 8½˝ (1G, 4G).

From the leftover ends of these strips, cut 32 squares 2½˝ × 2½˝ (2G, 3G).

MAKING THE BLOCKS

Seam allowances are ¼˝ unless otherwise indicated.

There are 16 blocks in this quilt, each made up of 4 sections.

1. To make Section 1, sew piece 1A to piece 1B. Add piece 1C. Sew 1F to 1E and add 1D. Sew unit A/B/C to unit D/E/F, and then add pieces 1G and 1H. Make a total of 16 Section 1's.

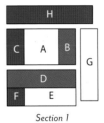

Section 1

2. To make Section 2, sew piece 2A to piece 2B. Add piece 2C. Sew unit A/B/C to piece 2D and add piece 2E. Sew piece 2F to piece 2G and add piece 2I. Sew piece 2H to one side of unit A/B/C/D/E and add unit F/G/I. Make a total of 16 Section 2's.

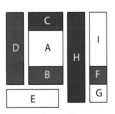

Section 2

3. To make Section 3, sew together in the same order as Section 2, except use the pieces designated for Section 3 and note the color placement in the diagram. Make a total of 16 Section 3's.

4. To make Section 4, sew together in the same order as Section 1, except use the pieces designated for Section 4 and note the color placement in the diagram. Make a total of 16 Section 4's.

5. Sew together 4 block sections to make a block. Repeat to make 16 twisted blocks.

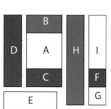

Section 3

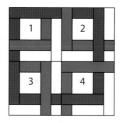

Section 4

PUTTING IT ALL TOGETHER

1. Refer to the assembly diagram to sew together the blocks into 4 rows of 4 blocks each.

2. Sew together the 4 rows.

Assembly diagram

QUILTING AND FINISHING

1. Mark the quilting design on the quilt top as described in How to Use the Quilting Patterns (page 23), or plan to free-motion quilt without marking.

2. Refer to Layering and Basting (page 17) to layer and baste the quilt top, batting, and backing.

3. Quilt as desired. Good quilting designs for this quilt are Clams (page 52) and Swirls (page 54). I quilted clams in white thread in all of the white background areas; on the purple and green strips, I quilted swirls.

4. Refer to Binding (page 121) to bind the quilt. Square it up as described in Squaring Up Your Quilt (page 23).

Finished size: 67⅞˝ × 67⅞˝

DAISY DROP

Designed by Kathleen Whiting and Natalia Bonner, made by Vickie Christensen and
Natalia Bonner, quilted by Natalia Bonner, and bound by Kathleen Whiting

*Three colors—two solids and a simple print—give this quilt
a bold, graphic look. Although you can use yardage to
make it, this design would easily lend itself to scraps. The
blocks are appliquéd and set on point.*

MATERIALS

Yardages are based on fabric that is at least 40˝ wide.

5 yards of white fabric

2 yards of purple fabric

2 yards of yellow fabric

⅝ yard of purple binding fabric

4¼ yards of backing fabric

2⅛ yards of 96˝-wide batting

CUTTING

Templates are on page 113 (E) and page 119 (H). Before cutting out the pieces to be appliquéd, refer to Appliqué Method (page 95).

Purple:

Cut 108 petals using template H.

Yellow:

Cut 120 petals using template H.

White:

Cut 13 squares 16½˝ × 16½˝.

Cut 2 squares 23⅞˝ × 23⅞˝; cut in half diagonally 2 times to make 8 side setting triangles.

Cut 2 squares 12¼˝ × 12¼˝; cut in half diagonally to make 4 corner setting triangles.

From the leftover fabric, cut 13 circles, 8 half-circles, and 4 quarter-circles using template E.

MAKING THE BLOCKS

This quilt is made up of 13 whole, 8 half-, and 4 quarter-blocks.

1. Refer to Appliqué Method (page 95). Prepare the purple appliqué pieces H as described.

2. Use a blanket or satin stitch to appliqué 6 purple F petals onto all 13 of the 16½˝ × 16½˝ blocks (Figure 1). Place the vertical petals first, and then add the others. To ensure exact placement, use the 60° marks on a quilter's ruler or a 60° triangular ruler to place the petals.

3. Referring to Figure 2 for placement, appliqué 6 yellow F petals onto all 13 of the 16½˝ × 16½˝ blocks.

4. Referring to Figure 3 for placement, appliqué 3 purple petals onto each of 4 side setting triangles. One petal is perpendicular to one short side of the triangle. Referring to Figure 3, reverse the placement for the remaining 4 side setting triangles to create mirror images setting triangles.

5. Referring to Figure 4 for placement, appliqué 2 purple petals onto 2 of the smaller corner triangles and 1 petal onto the other 2 corner setting triangles.

6. Referring to Figures 3 and 4 for placement, appliqué 3 yellow petals onto each of the 8 larger triangles. Appliqué 2 yellow petals onto 2 of the smaller corner triangles and 1 yellow petal onto the other 2 corner triangles.

7. Appliqué the white E circle onto the center of each full block (Figure 5). Appliqué the half-circles and quarter-circles onto the half- and quarter-blocks, respectively.

Figure 1

Figure 2

Figure 3

Figure 4

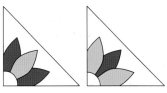

Figure 5

PUTTING IT ALL TOGETHER

Seam allowances are ¼˝ unless otherwise indicated.

1. The blocks are set on point. Sew together the blocks into 7 diagonal rows, as shown in the assembly diagram. Be sure to place the blocks so all the purple petals face in the same direction.

2. Sew together the diagonal rows.

Assembly diagram

QUILTING AND FINISHING

1. Mark the quilting design on the quilt top as described in How to Use the Quilting Patterns (page 23), or plan to free-motion quilt without marking.

2. Refer to Layering and Basting (page 17) to layer and baste the quilt top, batting, and backing.

3. Quilt as desired. Good quilting designs for this quilt are Swirls and Daisies (page 36), Double Pebbles (page 47), and Vine (page 84). I quilted swirls and daisies in white thread in the background, vines in yellow and purple in the flower petals, and double pebbles in the centers of the flowers.

4. Refer to Binding (page 121) to bind the quilt. Square it up as described in Squaring Up Your Quilt (page 23).

Pattern for Template H
Daisy Drop
Cut 108 purple and
120 yellow.

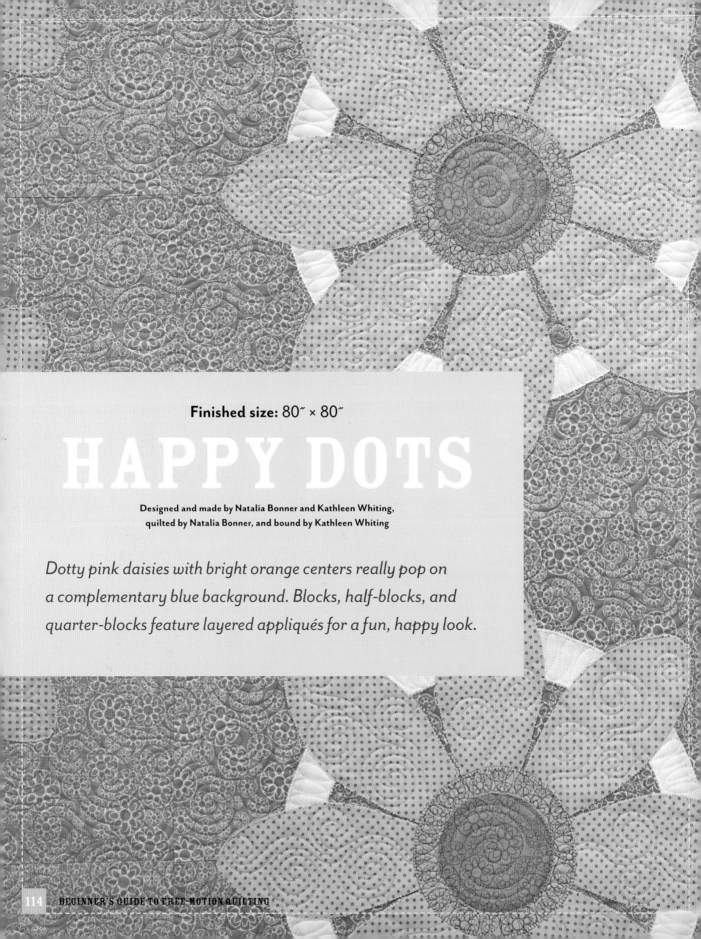

Finished size: 80˝ × 80˝

HAPPY DOTS

Designed and made by Natalia Bonner and Kathleen Whiting,
quilted by Natalia Bonner, and bound by Kathleen Whiting

*Dotty pink daisies with bright orange centers really pop on
a complementary blue background. Blocks, half-blocks, and
quarter-blocks feature layered appliqués for a fun, happy look.*

MATERIALS

Yardages are based on fabric that is at least 40˝ wide.

6½ yards of blue fabric

2⅝ yards of white fabric

3 yards of pink fabric

½ yard of green fabric

¼ yard of orange fabric

⅝ yard of binding fabric

7⅜ yards of backing fabric

2½ yards of 96˝-wide batting

CUTTING

Templates are on pages 119 and 120. Before cutting out the pieces to be appliquéd, refer to Appliqué Method (page 95).

Blue:

Cut 64 squares 10½˝ × 10½˝.

White:

Cut 64 pieces using template C.

Pink:

Cut 116 petals, 12 half-petals, and 12 reversed half-petals using template D.

Green:

Cut 11 circles, 8 half-circles, and 4 quarter-circles, using template E.

Orange:

Cut 11 circles, 8 half-circles, and 4 quarter-circles using template F.

MAKING THE BLOCKS

This quilt is made up of 11 whole, 8 half-, and 4 quarter-blocks.

For all appliqué pieces, refer to Appliqué Method (page 95), and use a blanket stitch or satin stitch to appliqué. After appliquéing the pieces in place, cut out the background fabric from behind the appliqués. When working with such dramatic colors, cutting out the background will result in a better product.

1. Appliqué a white piece C onto a corner of each of the 64 blue 10½˝ × 10½˝ squares (Figure 1).

Figure 1

2. Carefully trim the blue fabric from behind the appliqué, leaving a ¼˝ seam allowance. From the trimmed pieces of blue fabric, cut 64 pieces using template G.

Figure 2

3. Appliqué a blue piece G in the corner of each blue 10½˝ × 10½˝ square, on top of the appliquéd white piece (Figure 2).

4. Sew together 4 appliquéd squares from Step 3 into one block (Figure 3). Position the 4 smaller squares so that the white appliqués form a circle. Make a total of 11 blocks 20½˝ × 20½˝.

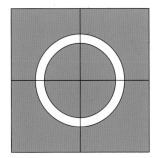

Figure 3

5. Sew together 2 appliquéd blue squares from Step 3 in pairs to make a total of 8 half-blocks 10½˝ × 20½˝ (Figure 4). You will have 4 small appliquéd quarter-blocks from Step 3 left over to use in the corners of the quilt.

6. Appliqué 8 pink D petals onto each block (Figure 5). To make the placement easier, place the horizontal and vertical petals first and then add the 4 remaining petals in between.

7. Appliqué 3 full D petals and 2 half-petals onto each half-block (Figure 6).

8. Appliqué 1 full D petal and 2 half-petals onto each quarter-block (Figure 7).

9. Appliqué a small orange full circle F onto a large green full circle E to make a total of 11. Repeat with each of the 8 half-circles and 4 quarter-circles.

10. Appliqué the orange/green circles onto the center of 11 blocks (Figure 8). Appliqué the orange/green half-circles to the 8 half-blocks and the orange/green quarter-circles to the 4 quarter-blocks (as pictured).

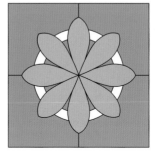

Figure 4

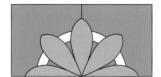

Figure 5

Figure 6

Figure 7

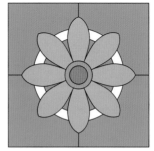

Figure 8

PUTTING IT ALL TOGETHER

Seam allowances are ¼˝ unless otherwise indicated.

1. Refer to the assembly diagram to sew the blocks into rows.

2. Sew the 5 rows together.

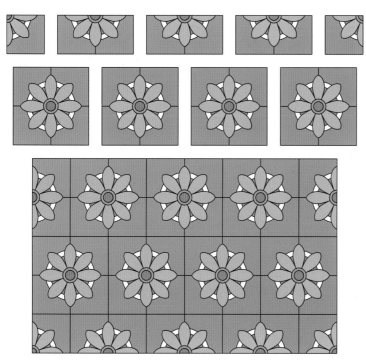

Assembly diagram

QUILTING AND FINISHING

1. Mark the quilting design on the quilt top as described in How to Use the Quilting Patterns (page 23), or plan to free-motion quilt without marking.

2. Refer to Layering and Basting (page 17) to layer and baste the quilt top, batting, and backing.

3. Quilt as desired. Good quilting designs for this quilt are Swirls (page 34), Ovals (page 67), and Vine (page 84). I quilted swirls in blue thread on the background and in orange thread on the orange flower centers. I then quilted ovals in white and green threads on the white and green appliqués. I quilted vines in pink thread on the flower petals.

4. Refer to Binding (page 121) to bind the quilt. Square it up as described in Squaring Up Your Quilt (page 23).

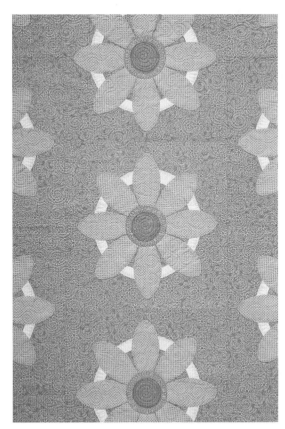

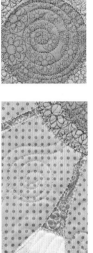

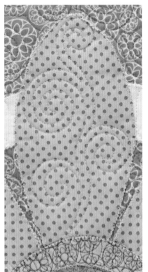

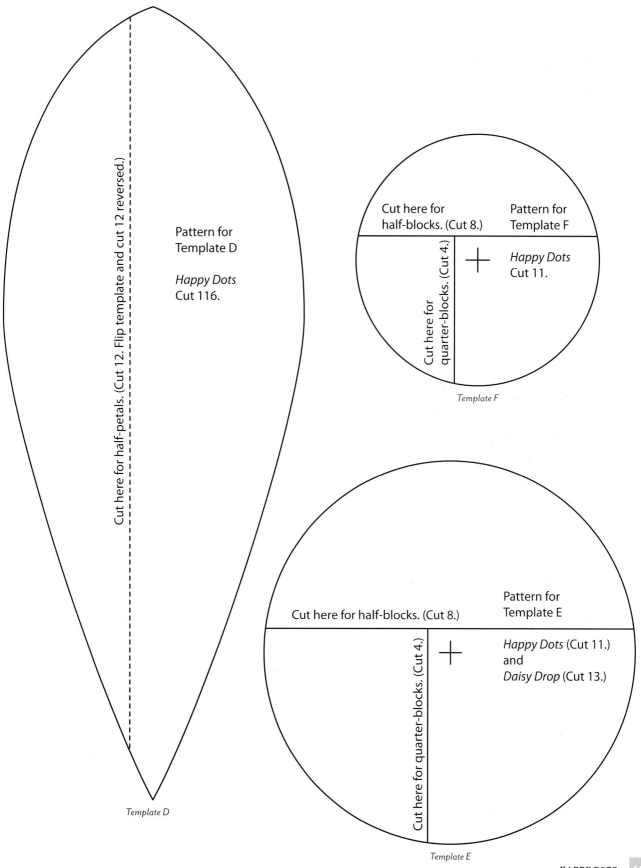

Cut here for half-petals. (Cut 12. Flip template and cut 12 reversed.)

Pattern for
Template D

Happy Dots
Cut 116.

Template D

Cut here for
half-blocks. (Cut 8.)

Pattern for
Template F

Cut here for quarter-blocks. (Cut 4.)

Happy Dots
Cut 11.

Template F

Cut here for half-blocks. (Cut 8.)

Pattern for
Template E

Cut here for quarter-blocks. (Cut 4.)

Happy Dots (Cut 11.)
and
Daisy Drop (Cut 13.)

Template E

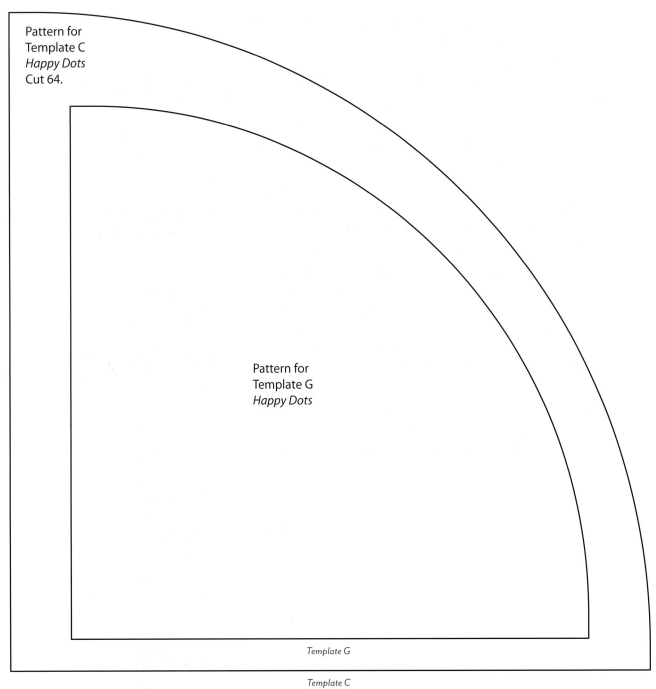

Pattern for
Template C
Happy Dots
Cut 64.

Pattern for
Template G
Happy Dots

Template G

Template C

BINDING

Trim excess batting and backing from the quilt so that they are even with the edges of the quilt top.

Double-Fold Straight-Grain Binding

If you want a ¼˝ finished binding, cut the binding strips 2˝ wide and piece them together with diagonal seams to make a continuous binding strip (Figure 1). Trim the seam allowance to ¼˝. Press the seams open (Figure 2).

Press the entire strip in half lengthwise with wrong sides together. With raw edges even, pin the binding to the front edge of the quilt a few inches away from the corner. Leave the first few inches of the binding unattached. Start sewing, using a ¼˝ seam allowance.

Stop ¼˝ away from the first corner (Figure 3) and backstitch one stitch. Lift the presser foot and needle. Rotate the quilt one-quarter turn. Fold the binding at a right angle so it extends straight above the quilt and the fold forms a 45° angle in the corner (Figure 4). Bring the binding strip down even with the edge of the quilt (Figure 5). Begin sewing at the folded edge. Repeat in the same manner at all corners.

Continue stitching until you are back near the beginning of the binding strip. See Finishing the Binding Ends (page 123) for tips on finishing and hiding the raw edges of the ends of the binding.

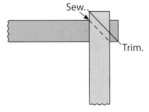

Sew.

Trim.

Figure 1

Figure 2

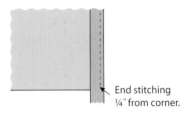

End stitching ¼˝ from corner.

Figure 3

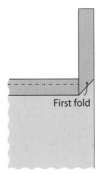

First fold

Figure 4

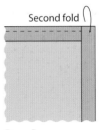

Second fold

Figure 5

Continuous Bias Binding

A continuous bias involves using a square sliced in half diagonally and then sewing the triangles together so that you continuously cut marked strips to make continuous bias binding. These same instructions can be used to cut bias for piping.

Cut the fabric for the bias binding or piping so it is a square. For example, if yardage is ½ yard, cut an 18˝ × 18˝ square. Cut the square in half diagonally, creating two triangles. Sew these triangles together as shown, using a ¼˝ seam allowance. Press the seam open (Figure 6).

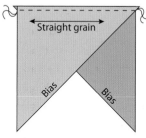

Figure 6

Using a ruler, mark the parallelogram created by the two triangles with lines spaced the width you need to cut the bias. Cut about 5˝ along the first line (Figure 7).

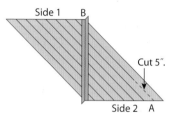

Figure 7

Join Side 1 and Side 2 to form a tube. The raw edge at line A will align with the raw edge at B. This will allow the first line to be offset by a strip width. Pin the raw edges with right sides together, making sure that the lines match (Figure 8). Sew with a ¼˝ seam allowance. Press the seam open. Cut along the drawn lines, creating one continuous strip.

Press the entire strip in half lengthwise with wrong sides together.

Place the binding on the quilt as described in Double-Fold Straight-Grain Binding (page 121).

See Finishing the Binding Ends (page 123) for tips on finishing and hiding the raw edges of the ends of the binding.

Figure 8

Finishing the Binding Ends

METHOD 1

After stitching around the quilt, fold under the beginning tail of the binding strip by ¼˝ so that the raw edge will be inside the binding after it is turned to the back of the quilt. Place the end tail of the binding strip over the beginning folded end. Continue to attach the binding and stitch slightly beyond the starting stitches. Trim the excess binding. Fold the binding over the raw edges to the quilt back and hand stitch, mitering the corners.

METHOD 2

See our blog entry at ctpubblog.com, search for "invisible seam," then scroll down to "Quilting Tips: Completing a Binding with an Invisible Seam."

Fold the ending tail of the binding back on itself where it meets the beginning binding tail. From the fold, measure and mark the cut width of the binding strip. Cut the ending binding tail to this measurement (Figure 9). For example, if your binding is cut 2⅛˝ wide, measure from the fold on the ending tail of the binding by 2⅛˝ and cut the binding tail to this length.

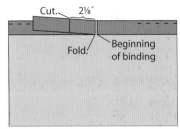

Figure 9

Open both tails. Place one tail on top of the other tail at right angles, right sides together. Mark a diagonal line from corner to corner and stitch on the line (Figure 10). Check that you've done it correctly and that the binding fits the quilt; then trim the seam allowance to ¼˝. Press open.

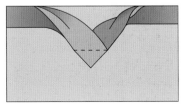

Figure 10

Refold the binding and stitch this binding section in place on the quilt. Fold the binding over the raw edges to the quilt back and hand stitch.

QUILTING PATTERNS

On the following pages, you will find 50 full-size patterns. You can use water-soluble marker to either trace your chosen pattern onto the quilt top or cut out the pattern and draw around it. For details on how to copy or trace the patterns, see How to Use the Quilting Patterns (page 23). These patterns are intended for you to use when practicing quilting. When you are ready to quilt your actual quilt top, you can draw or trace the pattern onto one area of the top, and use the pattern as a stitching guide to get you started. When you get the motion going, you can free-motion quilt over the entire top.

Single loops

Double loops

Loops and daisies

Loops and poppies

Loops and leaves

Loops and hearts

Loops and stars

Swirls

Swirls and daisies

Swirls and poppies

Swirls and half-daisies

Swirls and half-poppies

Feathers

Flames

Circles

Rounded feathers

Pointed feathers

Double feathers

BEGINNER'S GUIDE TO FREE-MOTION QUILTING

Double-spine feathers

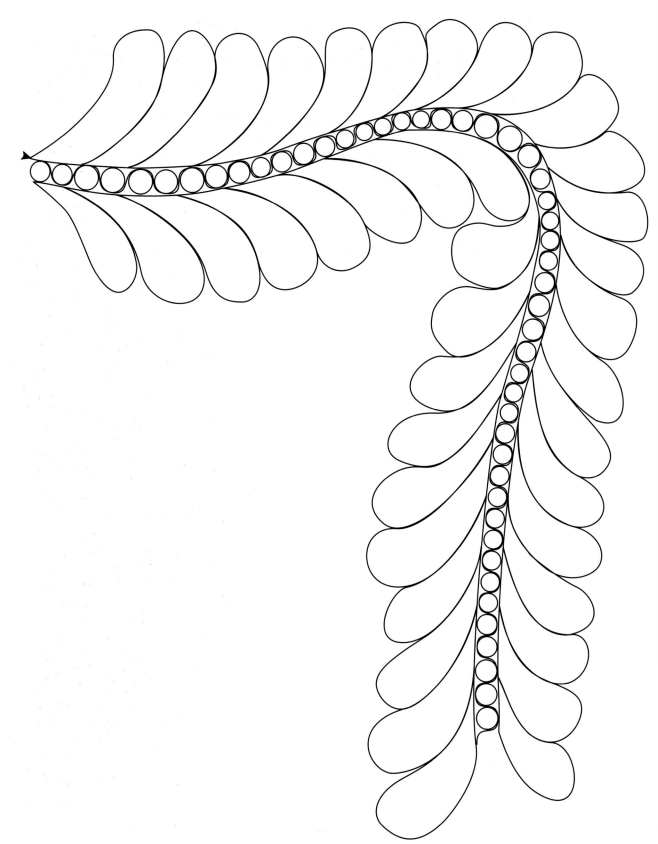

Filled-spine feathers

Swirl feathers

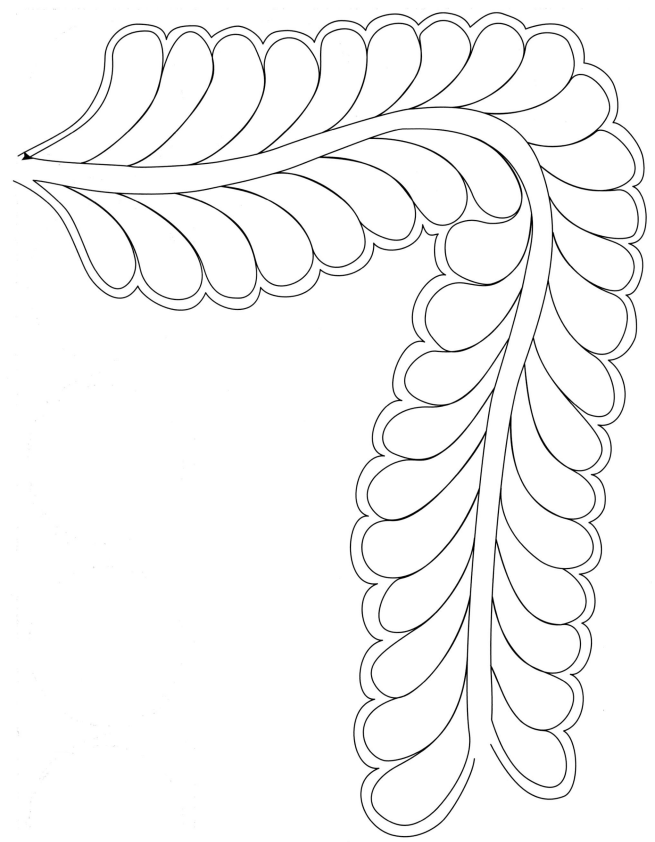

Echoed feathers

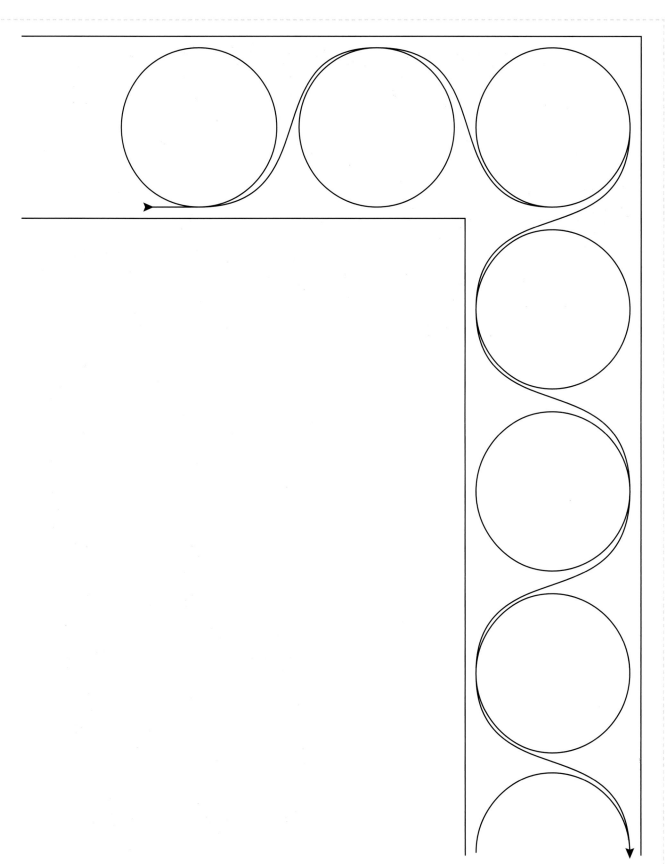

Single circles

Double circles

Triple circles

Swirls

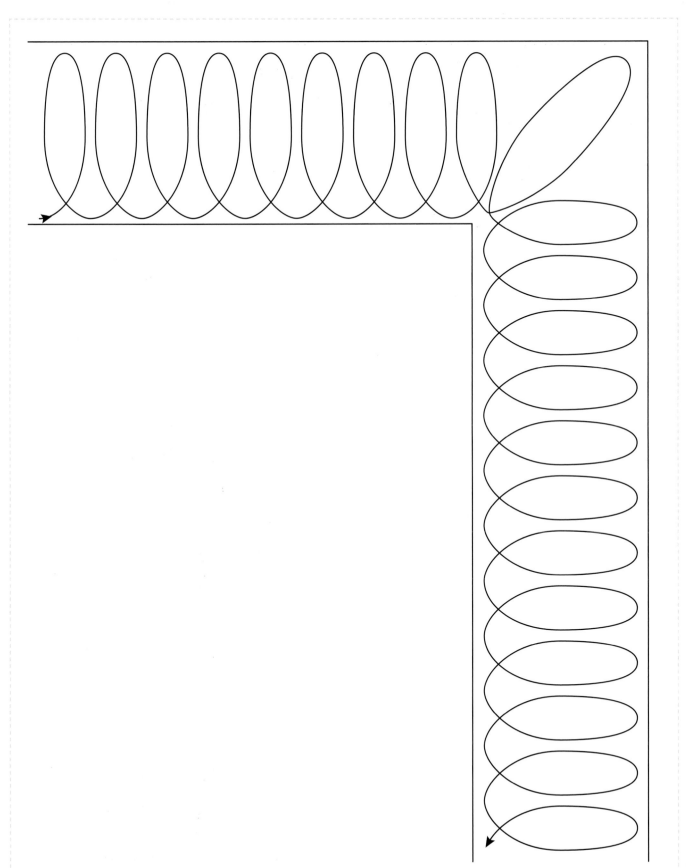

Ovals

Daisies

Poppies

Echoed daisies

Leaves

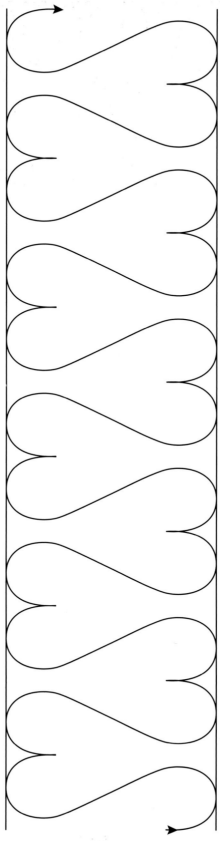

Hearts

BEGINNER'S GUIDE TO FREE-MOTION QUILTING

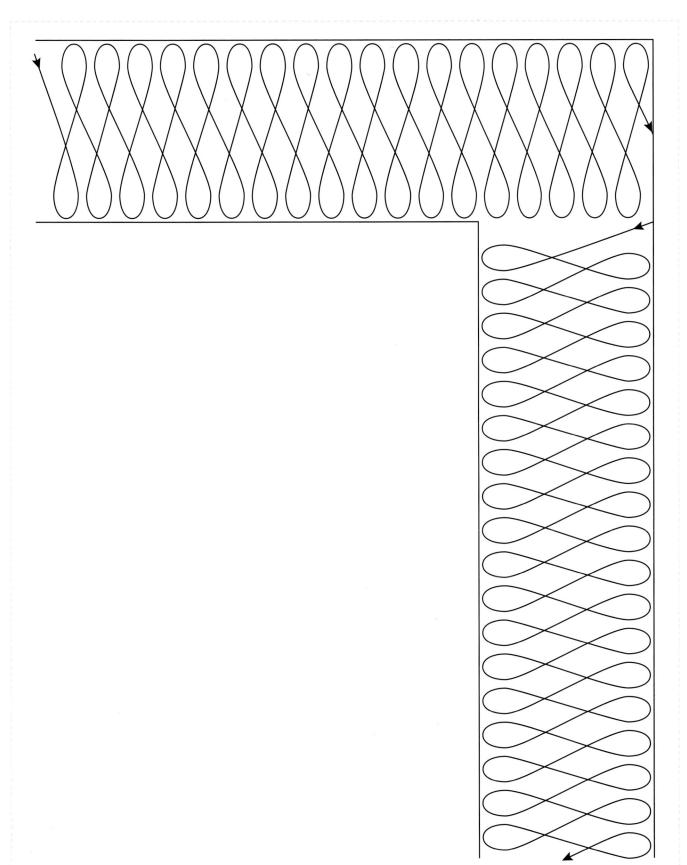

Figure 8's

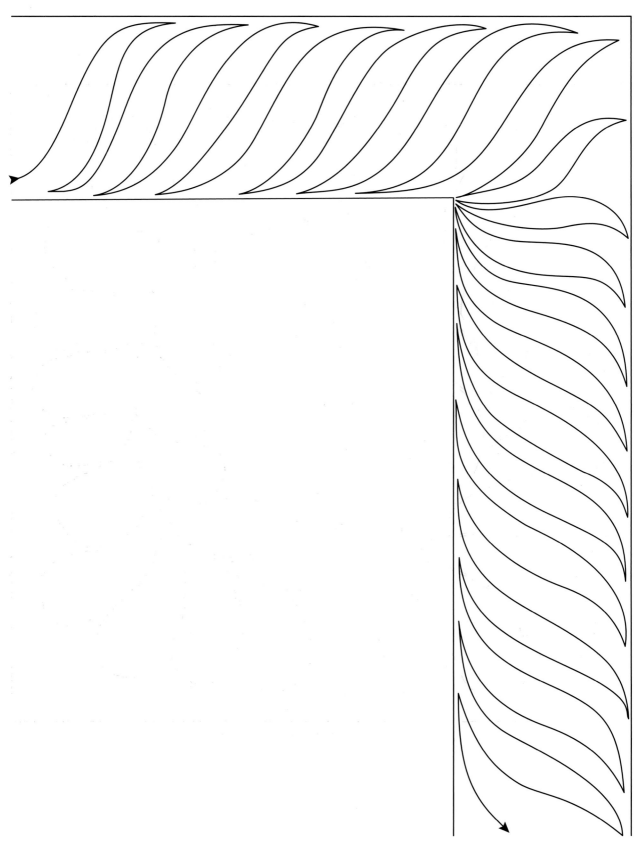

S's

Single feathers

Double feathers

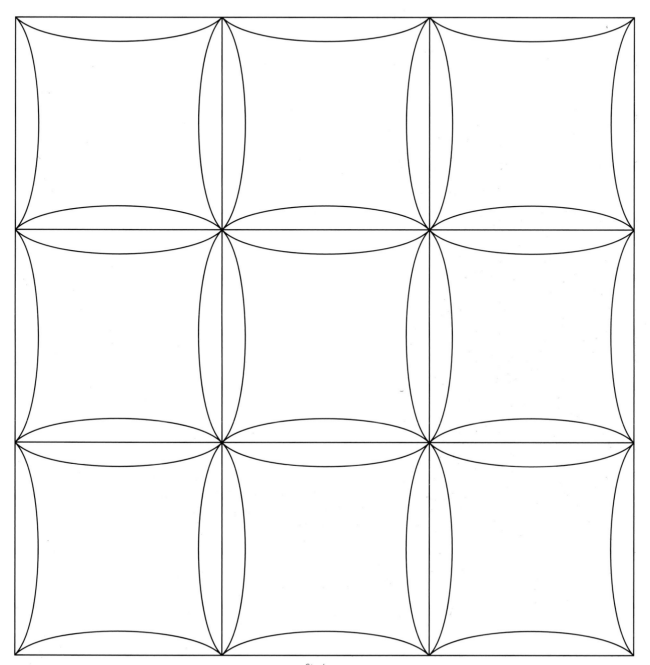

Single arcs

Double arcs

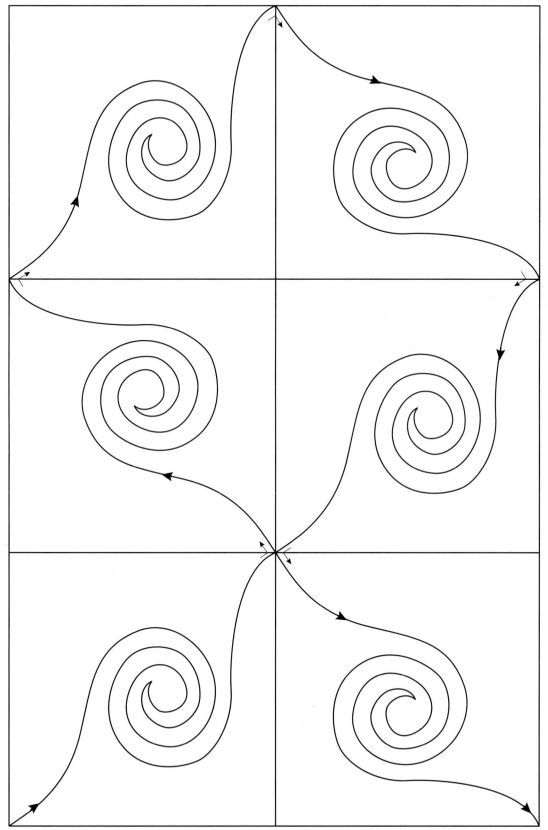

Swirls

Flower

Vine

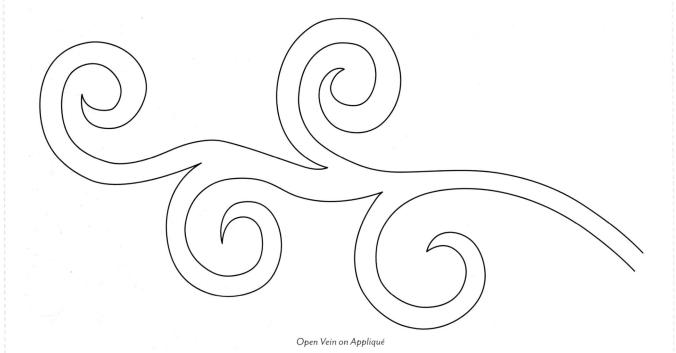

Open Vein on Appliqué

Single pebbles: Begin at the side center and work your way around the piece, connecting the circles as you go.

Double pebbles: Begin at the side center and work your way around the piece, connecting the circles as you go.

C pebbles: Begin at the side center and work your way around the piece, connecting the circles as you go.

Cobblestones

Wood grain

Clams

Swirls

Microstipple

Resources

BATTING

Quilters Dream Batting
quiltersdream.com

NEEDLES AND THREAD

Superior Threads
superiorthreads.com

HIGH-QUALITY FABRIC

Can be found at many mom-and-pop fabric shops and also online. Most manufacturers will have a list of retail shops where their fabrics can be purchased. Most of these shops also sell notions, such as Machingers gloves and safety pins.

Fabrics and materials in this book were provided by:

Moda Fabrics
unitednotions.com

Riley Blake Designs
rileyblakedesigns.com

Robert Kaufman Company
robertkaufman.com

Hobbs Bonded Fibers
hobbsbatting.com

Quilters Dream Batting
quiltersdreambatting.com

ABOUT THE AUTHOR

Photo by Whinee North

Natalia Whiting Bonner has enjoyed piecing quilt tops for more than twenty years. She learned how to quilt on her conventional home machine. She felt good about it, but decided that if she really wanted to take her quilting to the next level, she needed to invest in a longarm machine. In 2007, when she was pregnant with her daughter, she got the crazy idea to quit her job as a dental assistant and become a longarm quilter. Without really knowing what a longarm machine was, she spent a day at a longarm dealer's shop and walked out after purchasing a Gammill machine. Natalia's passion for quilting and being creative has grown each day since.

Shortly after her purchase, Natalia began blogging at piecenquilt.blogspot.com, and blogging became her connection with other quilters and fellow work-at-home moms. By 2009, her quilting business had grown, and it was time to leave the tiny, poorly lit bedroom where she had been doing all her quilting. Natalia moved into a studio at her parents' home, and with the inspiration of her mother, Kathleen Whiting, she has realized that the sky is the limit.

Whether it's working on an intense show quilt or a simple baby quilt, Natalia has become a real quilting addict. She has won numerous awards for her work and has been featured on Moda Bake Shop, in *Quiltmaker Magazine* and *American Patchwork & Quilting Magazine*, and in books such as *Fresh Fabric Treats: 16 Yummy Projects to Sew from Jelly Rolls, Layer Cakes & More with Your Favorite Moda Bakeshop Designers* and *Modern Blocks: 99 Quilt Blocks from Your Favorite Designers* (both from Stash Books, an imprint of C&T Publishing).

stashBOOKS

fabric arts for a handmade lifestyle

If you're craving beautiful authenticity in a time of mass-production...Stash Books is for you. Stash Books is a line of how-to books celebrating fabric arts for a handmade lifestyle. Backed by C&T Publishing's solid reputation for quality, Stash Books will inspire you with contemporary designs, clear and simple instructions, and engaging photography.

www.stashbooks.com